MW01289126

Soul's Journey

Discovering Your Heart's Desire

To Renee,

May your Soul's journey bring you every desire within your heart.

Rev. Dr. Becky Rector

Rev. Dr. Becky Rector, MDiv

BALBOA
PRESS
A DIVISION OF HAY HOUSE

Balboa Press books may be ordered through booksellers or by contacting:

Balboa Press
A Division of Hay House
1663 Liberty Drive
Bloomington, IN 47403
www.balboapress.com
1 (877) 407-4847

Because of the dynamic nature of the Internet, any web addresses or links contained in
this book may have changed since publication and may no longer be valid. The views
expressed in this work are solely those of the author and do not necessarily reflect the
views of the publisher, and the publisher hereby disclaims any responsibility for them.

The author of this book does not dispense medical advice or prescribe the use
of any technique as a form of treatment for physical, emotional, or medical
problems without the advice of a physician, either directly or indirectly. The
intent of the author is only to offer information of a general nature to help you
in your quest for emotional and spiritual well-being. In the event you use any
of the information in this book for yourself, which is your constitutional right,
the author and the publisher assume no responsibility for your actions.

This book is a work of non-fiction. Unless otherwise noted, the author and the publisher
make no explicit guarantees as to the accuracy of the information contained in this book
and in some cases, names of people and places have been altered to protect their privacy.

Scriptures taken from King James Version

Any people depicted in stock imagery provided by Thinkstock are models,
and such images are being used for illustrative purposes only.
Certain stock imagery © Thinkstock.

Print information available on the last page.

ISBN: 978-1-5043-8733-0 (sc)
ISBN: 978-1-5043-8735-4 (hc)
ISBN: 978-1-5043-8734-7 (e)

Library of Congress Control Number: 2017913692

Balboa Press rev. date: 09/11/2017

Thank you, Divine Source, God, for all the love that continues to bless us all. Thank you for making this all possible.

From the depth of my being, thank you to my incredibly loving spouse, Rocky R. Rector, for your love, support, strength and consistent encouragement. Thank you for the amazing life you give us. This book is dedicated to you and our marriage. I love you eternally.

Thank you to my mom and dad, for being the best parents to me. Thank you for always believing in me. I love you.

Thank you to my minister and teacher, Rev. Dr. Linda Marie Nelson for helping to make so much possible. Especially for blessing and officiating my marriage to Rocky.

Professional and heartfelt gratitude to Rev. Tanya Tiger and DeAnne Moore for the hours you gifted me in helping make this possible.

To my teachers Rev. Dr. Robert Estling, Rev. Dr. Sherry Gustafson, Rev. Dee Mitchell and Rev. Jane "Weed" Roy, thank you for the profound teachings you have each given me.

Table of Contents

Introduction

Within these pages I hope to impress upon you the innate ability each of us has to make manifest the life we most desire to live. I intend to illustrate my theory by presenting personal experiences and case studies, along with methodologies used by various spiritual practitioners. This journey begins in childhood with the seeming "magic" of our imaginations and ends with us uncovering our heart's desire and putting our intentions into action.

Most of us have fond memories of playing pretend when we were children. Even in the most challenging of childhoods there are moments of wishing upon a star, or playing with toys and friends. In the past, before technology existed in the way it does today, we were gifted the freedom of our imagination. In our pretend play, we dreamed big. We may have been a super hero helping a person in need or a teacher making a difference. Perhaps we were a romantic prince or princess or a loving king or queen. We may have been a famous rock star, an actor or actress, or a champion athlete. Perhaps we were more nature oriented in our pretend world, choosing to become magical fairies, or unicorns. The options were limitless.

Unfortunately, as we aged, our families, teachers, and other mentors guided us to a different pretend world—a world we were told was the "real world." In this real world, we needed to get good grades so we would eventually graduate high school and go to college. Once we achieved that milestone, we were told, we would have to get a good-paying job, buy a house, buy a car, get married, and have children. Often the dreams we once had of becoming famous, or of making a difference in the world, fell by the wayside because we needed to grow up.

As we grew up, we got very lost in this so-called real world. We became consumed by responsibilities to our family members, friends, employers, and more. We had bills to pay, and we were pressured to succeed and to secure a stable future. We were encouraged to make our health a priority. As adults we find that our dreams have not only faded into the background, they have disappeared from our consciousness.

Interestingly, as the dreams of our youth continue to fade away, we also see changes in our health. We feel disconnected from our lives. A sense of discontentment takes over, even when we have everything we were taught we needed to be happy. We constantly search for something without knowing what that something even is. We may feel lost and alone. Many of us receive diagnoses of depression, anxiety disorders, and other stress-related problems. After we have spent some time living this life and continuing to feel that something is missing, we embark upon a journey to find ourselves.

Years ago, as I was living a life similar to what I just described, I cultivated a practice of daily meditation. This came after I became highly stressed and was diagnosed with hypertension. I started taking blood pressure medication just a few weeks after I turned thirty. The thought I had after receiving that diagnosis was, *Why am I already beginning a life of unhealthiness at thirty! That's way too young!* A dear friend, and at the time my boss, asked me one day how I was doing. I responded, as a good employee, by updating him on my sales goals and quotas, and what I had in my pipeline. His kind and gentle heart interrupted my flow, stating, "No, Becky. How are you doing? Are you taking care of yourself spiritually?" I knew the true answer was no. That day was the first day of my daily meditation practice.

My meditations began as simple ten-minute periods of sitting outside in the woods near my home. I would just close my eyes and breathe. This ten minutes quickly became one to one and a half hours. During these meditations, I began to reconnect with my heart. I remembered what I really "wanted to be when I grew up." I recalled what I used to imagine for myself in my pretending days. I always wanted to be a teacher and to help people. It's what I was most called to do. When I was a child, my friends and I would play "school," and I was always the teacher. We also organized various clubs. The most successful one was the Don't Worry Be Happy Club. We would meet every week in the basement of the home I grew up in. We paid weekly dues of fifty cents each, which over time would add up to be enough for an outing to a movie or something else fun. With every club we created, I was always voted as the president. My best friend was vice president, and the other girls were elected as the secretary and the treasurer.

Remembering this draw to teaching, I began to really focus on the parts of my dreams that dealt with being a teacher and helping people. When I looked closely at my current life, I realized that I wasn't living my dreams. I was the sales representative for a third-party ultrasound service company. I was also helping my partner start her commercial cleaning business. I was paying bills, and I was going further into debt. Any dreams I once had were long gone, lost in the ocean of "real life" responsibilities.

One day during meditation I asked, "What is my heart's desire?" The message I received helped me understand that what I wanted for my life was to teach people about spiritual things, such as meditation. I wanted to help others connect to their heart's desire, and to bring more peace into their lives. That was over five years ago. Today, through teaching workshops and working with various clients via my spiritual counseling and coaching business, Soul Journeys, I have discovered how significant living our heart's desire is to all of our journeys, and how vital it is for each of us to embark upon this journey of discovery.

In my workshops I often ask, "What did you imagine when you played pretend as a child?" I guide the participants into a meditation and have them focus on a fond memory of their childhood. In evaluating and discussing these meditations, I have found that what we imagined during those "play pretend" years were signposts pointing toward aspects of who we really are, at our core. Participants tell me about pretending to be teachers, famous writers, musicians, artists, or athletes. When people share, especially when I know a little about them before the event, I see how those childhood pretend identities and dreams have foretold the roles they actually fulfill today.

As I began to learn more, I pondered about what this world would be like if Maya Angelo had not followed her true heart's desire. Where would we be today without the O Network, through which Oprah Winfrey inspires millions of people every day because she followed her heart's desire? I realized a truth in this: The world is waiting for each of us to connect with, and to *live*, our *heart's desire*. It isn't a whimsical fantasy. There is a reason this desire exists within our hearts, and a reason we follow it. The question remains, though: How do we discover our heart's desire? I will discuss that question in more detail in the chapters that follow.

After meditating and realizing that my real life was far from what I had imagined it would be when I was a child, I knew that my heart's desire was to teach people about various spiritual thoughts and methodologies, and to help others find happiness within themselves. I didn't know how I would make this happen, and every fear I could imagine rose up to greet me. I thought, *I can go back to school, but I can't quit my job too. I have bills to pay.* I considered going to the Florida School of Massage, thinking, *I can become a massage therapist, and maybe teach there one day.* I felt drawn there, so I believed that, perhaps, that would work out for me. While the classes would fit around my work schedule, the cost just didn't feel right. I learned the true power that came with being fully aware of the heart's desire. Now that I knew my heart's desire, there wasn't an excuse in the world that would prevent me from manifesting it divinely in my life.

Despite recognizing that I had reconnected with my heart's desire, I let go of the dream and focused my energy back toward my real life work. Yet, the desire grew more and more intense. Then a divine meeting occurred while I was attending a networking event. I met a ray of sunshine who invited me to a workshop at her center. After I attended, we became friends. One day, not long after the workshop, she asked to do an exchange-of-service with me. In exchange for cleaning her apartment (I owned a cleaning company at the time), she offered me four sessions of hypnotherapy. After the first session, she mentioned someone named Rev. Bob and told me that I needed to meet him. After the second session, she asked if I had ever been to the Seraphim Center. She said that "my people" were there. After the third session, she gave me Rev. Bob's number and insisted that I call him and enroll in the ministry program.

I remember thinking, *Me, a minister? No way.* I couldn't even image that. But, within a few weeks, I was enrolled in Rev. Bob's next class. The phenomenal realization came when I learned that the Seraphim Center, Rev. Bob's church, had been meeting at the Florida School of Massage for the past year. I knew immediately the reason I had been led to consider classes there. I met Rev. Bob and connected with the Seraphim Center.

I didn't feel ready to release the security blanket of my job or the illusions I held that sustained my fears. I enrolled in the classes thinking I could complete them while maintaining my job. All the while, my heart continued to pull me more and more toward focusing on the ministry and teaching. Within a year's time, I was laid off from my sales job. It's funny how the Spirit works. This is a point where the concept of "illusion of control" can show up. I found myself, for a moment, lost in this illusion. I was upset about losing my job, afraid of what might happen, and doing all I could to fix things.

But actually my life had shifted, and that meant that things that didn't align with my heart's desire were falling away. When I learned of the fear-based thought process I was having, and that it could impede the flow of what good might come, I shifted back to my heart space. It then became clear that when we connect to our heart's desire, things shift into place. When these shifts take place, we can either go with the flow by allowing the Universe to shift things for us, or we can take a leap of faith and make the required shifts to reach our goals. Either way, once we've identified our heart's desire and set our awareness on achieving it, everything will unfold to make it happen. It's destined to manifest this way, and I think it's great!

Over and over again, I have had many experiences as I've connected with my heart's desire (which evolves as I evolve), and I either observe the Universe shift so everything falls into place, or I take a leap of faith. These experiences are not always easy because they require change. Change is incredible. Change is wonderful. Change can also be difficult, and it can be scary because it makes us step outside our comfort zone, which forces us to face the unknown.

As you will see in these pages, I faced change often, and although these experiences of taking a leap of faith were rarely easy, they were powerful. Included in these changes was the unexpected rise of a deep longing to move to South Carolina. My heart's desire remained focused on teaching and helping others, but it now included a pull toward relocating to the Carolinas.

Although my entire real life was based in Florida—I was in the tenth year of my relationship, the ninth year of owning my home, and all of my family lived in Florida—I could not deny this draw to be in the Carolinas. I continuously felt guided to be there, and I would find reasons to travel there for training. The very moment I crossed the border from Georgia to South Carolina, I could breathe. That's how I knew I needed to relocate. As I will discuss more in depth in these chapters, my life was on a trajectory with what some would call destiny. Without my conscious awareness, the Universe was aligning the opportunities I needed to achieve my heart's desire, and I was along for the ride.

On December 21, 2012, I received a job offer while I was visiting in South Carolina. For those who may not recall, December 21, 2012, was the day said to be the end of the Mayan calendar (Braden 2009, 57). Many predicted that it would be the end of the world as we knew it. For me, this prophecy was truly unfolding. My world, as I knew it, was now coming to an end. While I had gained an enormous amount of experience after my beloved teacher, Rev. Bob, passed away and left me in charge of the Seraphim Center, I knew that, ultimately, the center was not where I was in life. When I received a job offer that would require me to relocate to South Carolina, I knew that it was an opportunity I simply couldn't turn down. I chose this time to take a leap of faith. I returned home to Florida and had a 2012 kind of Christmas. I use that phrase, because there had been a great many books and discussions about the Mayan calendar prophecy, predicting the world would come to an end on December 21, 2012. For me, my world *had* come to an end. Doors were closing immediately all around me. I tried to maintain my already failing relationship, but soon realized that, inevitably, this chapter of my life was coming to a close. I contacted members of the community in Florida, which I had grown to love, seeking a place to stay during this transition, only to be turned away time after time. The only offers of support I received came from people in the Carolinas, and my soon-to-be ex. This wasn't an easy time for me. Despite these difficult times, I could not shake a deep inner knowing that everything would all work out. I could do this fearlessly, or it would fall into place a little later. Either way, it would be.

I obtained such wisdom. I quickly discovered that what awaited me on the other side of these difficult experiences was heaven on earth. I arrived in the Carolinas and moved into the sweetest little cottage. There was a swing on the porch that overlooked a beautiful lake with a white bridge and a gazebo. There were Canadian geese all around. I found it interesting that this was the vision I'd had during the numerous meditations

I guided people through, but that's another story altogether. Just when I thought, *How could life get any better than this?* it did. I connected with my soul mate, my true love, and today we are happily married and living in a beautiful cabin in the mountains of the northern part of South Carolina.

So now that I have recounted some of my personal experiences in obtaining my heart's desire (there is much more to come), I'd like to provide additional information about how to recognize your own heart's desire and a meditation to help you make this discovery.

CHAPTER 1

Recognizing Your Heart's Desire

Many people have asked themselves, *What is my heart's desire?* This question can be confusing. Perhaps you arrived at a point when you felt confident in what your heart's desire looked like. You may have even started making the choice to go after it, whatever it is, only to have something get in your way, maybe more than once. This barrier that always seems to pop up may have manifested as fear, either your own or that of a loved one, that pulled you away from your decision. This fear of the unknown may have forced you to stay in your current situation. No matter how this barrier manifested, it seemed to get in your way every time.

Now, some people may believe this interference is a sign from the utmost. Or perhaps they believe that, by staying in their current situation, they will find a new happiness that will lead to contentment. So which is the true heart's desire? The answer is simple: It's the one that, when you see yourself obtaining it, gives you the most joy and happiness. It's the one that makes your heart race. When you experience those reactions, you will recognize that you have found your heart's desire.

The process that occurs when you connect to your heart's desire and then affirm that it is what you truly want is amazing. Life shifts, and things change. It sounds remarkable, right? Well, let's not get ahead of ourselves. There is a lot more to this process, and I want to begin with a meditation to assist you in uncovering your heart's desire. I will follow this with some basic background information to help you fully embrace the understanding of living your heart's desire. Believe me when I say that the cliché about truth being stranger than fiction is … well, true. Once you are locked in to your heart's desire, your life will never be the same.

So please get comfortable and let us begin our journey from a place of love. We will begin with the heart's desire meditation.

CHAPTER 2

Heart's Desire Meditation

Settle yourself comfortably in a quiet place. Close your eyes for a moment. Take in a deep breath and relax. Breathe in and count to four. Hold the breath and count to four. Now, breathe out and count to four. Do this twice. Now return to a normal breathing pattern.

Bring your awareness to your head and allow your head to simply relax. Bring your awareness to your shoulders and arms and feel them relax. Now, bring your awareness to your back and allow it to relax. Bring your awareness to your chest and then your abdomen and feel your upper torso relax. Bring your awareness down to your legs and feet. Allow your legs and feet to simply relax.

Now imagine you are walking down a beautiful path in nature. The temperature is perfect, and there is beauty all around you. The sounds of the birds are like a beautiful song. The sky is a bright blue, and the colors around you are brilliant and vivid. Notice up ahead there is a beautiful waterfall flowing and a perfect space where you can sit and relax. As you sit comfortably there, take in a loving breath from your heart. Now imagine in front of you the image of your heart. Feel his or her presence. Ask, "What is my truest heart's desire?" Listen for the answer.

As you breathe in the answer, feel the loving presence around you. Feel the powerful energy of love surround you. Experience what it would feel like to live in your heart's desire. Allow that energy to grow around you.

Now, while maintaining that feeling, thank your heart for sharing this gift with you. Continue to carry that feeling with you as you begin your journey back. As you retrace your steps back down that beautiful trail in nature, feel the sense of gratitude for this time. Hold that love in your heart and, when you are ready, open your eyes.

Write down everything you experienced. What is your heart's desire? How did you feel about being in the presence of your heart's desire? Did it excite you? Did it place a smile on your face? Is there a part of you that felt childlike again, as if you were tapping into your imagination? Is there a part of you that said, "I wish," "If only I had …," "That would be great if …"

Welcome to your heart's desire!

If you did not understand clearly your heart's desire, let go of any discouragement and simply continue to practice the meditation. You will understand it in perfect divine time.

CHAPTER 3

Living the Spark of Divinity We Are

Within each and every one of us is a powerful spark of divinity. We came into this life experience destined for greatness. We should live a life of abundance, one in which we thrive. Within each and every one of us exists a clear and divine blueprint for the unfolding of our lives' paths. It has been there since the dawn of our existence. All the books, workshops, teachings, and life experiences are simply guideposts placed along our paths to aid us in aligning with the life of divinity we live.

Each of us enters this life with powerful gifts. We knew of these gifts as children, but for various reasons we may have suppressed them as we transitioned into adulthood. All are part of the blueprint of who we are. Without exception, absolutely everything has happened and is happening for a purpose. This includes the good things, the challenging things, and everything between.

This concept can be difficult to understand, especially when tragedy strikes or we witness a senseless act of violence.

If only we could pull back and see our entire lives stretched out before us, we would see how everything is connected and aligned just for us. It would all make sense. For now, we must trust and learn the lessons as they come.

Looking back at our lives, we can see there is a thread running through every experience, and this thread reminds us of the spark and the true essence of who we are. If we simply focus our attention, we can see it.

As you read this, I know you sense it strongly. It's part of who you are. It is who you are. Each and every one of us is a beautiful spark of divinity. It is now time to ignite your spark and allow it to shine light onto the blueprint of your life.

Within each of us exists the potential to be like our idols: Oprah, Wayne Dyer, Gandhi, Melissa Etheridge, Tarzan, Superman—anyone. Within me is the most amazing person, and I am destined for greatness. I also know that within you is the most spectacular person and that you too are destined for greatness. The question is: do you believe this to be true? It is vital that you realize this truth, for this where your power lives.

Within us all exists a desire that resonates from our hearts. This desire can be found in what deeply fascinates us in the subjects we read and in what we internally long to experience. Unfortunately, we often find that our current circumstances oppose what our hearts desire to make manifest. Our current life circumstances simply do not seem to yield this desired experience, and an internal struggle may ensue between what we desire and what our current circumstances require of us. This incongruence between what is and what we desire to experience can lead to turmoil. Relief comes when we discover this powerful truth: within each of us exists a blueprint—a map that guides our direction.

Some people, for various reasons, make the choice to stay within their current life circumstances. Over time, that longing within us continues to get louder and louder. Soon it becomes so loud that our life circumstances begin to be shaken up. The job becomes more difficult, the relationship becomes nearly unbearable, or the body manifests illnesses. All of these are indicators that it is time to make a change. The lives we have been living are no longer serving us; maybe they never were. Now the lives we live—the ones we would thrive in—are calling out to us. They're calling us to align with our hearts' desires and fully step into the lives we wish to thrive in. Are you ready to join me on a journey of discovery, the journey to uncover your heart's desire?

Every morning, I spend time in meditation as a way to prepare my being to write the words in my book. I want to inspire each and every human being on this earth to align with his or her heart's truest desire and to live every moment from that perspective. When we can do this, I know we will have cocreated heaven on earth. I know this personally because I have experienced glimpses of heaven on earth by taking a leap of faith toward that which is within my own heart.

A disclaimer here: Following our hearts' desires defies logical and rational understanding. To truly take a leap of faith toward your desire means that you must be ready and willing to toss out the spreadsheet budget, put aside the daily planner, and hit the pause button on the repeating litany of limiting thoughts that run through your head.

Begin here: Place your hands over your heart and breathe seven breaths, focusing them toward your heart. Now, visualize the life you truly desire to live. Allow yourself to feel this vision, and carry this feeling with you throughout your day. You will discover that, by doing this simple activity each day, divinely inspired action steps will appear.

How will you recognize a divinely inspired action? You will know by the excitement you feel in your heart. The sensation may be simple or complex, but you will feel it, and you will know the action is the right step to take.

It's important to note that everyone's journey is different. Some people may be filled with nervous excitement as they take their first steps, while others may feel scared as they step outside their comfort zones. Regardless of how you feel when you begin, take that first step. It is spectacular here in heaven on earth—truly.

CHAPTER 4

The Four Keys to Living Divine Consciousness

In this section, I will discuss four "keys" that act as simple reminders of how to live in alignment with the Divine. They are as follows:

1. Be centered in the heart.
2. Release the care of how.
3. Play with possibilities using childhood wonder.
4. Be in a receptive state.

Living in alignment with the Divine assists us in staying connected to our heart center. When in our heart space, we are no longer in contrast with the Divine's plan or, as commonly referred to, God's plan. We are in perfect alignment with God's plan, which we will find is in alignment with what we truly desire. Being connected to the divine manifestations of our hearts' desires become effortless, fast, and fun.

At this point in my life, through all of my research, studies, and personal experiences, I believe that heaven can absolutely be experienced on earth. The Bible teaches that the kingdom of heaven is within us: "Neither shall they say, Lo here! or, lo there! for, behold the kingdom of God is within you" (Luke 17:21 King James Version). If the kingdom of heaven is within me, then isn't that where my heart's desires come from? If the belief is that we are divine consciousness being physically expressed through human form—a physical manifestation of the Divine/God—then within me is the desire to express heaven on earth.

So, what is divine consciousness, and why is there a desire to live it? In every workshop I have ever done, a thread of similarity in expressed heart's desire unites the attendees. The thread is to be happy and experience the sensation of soaring through life. During these workshops, just as when any of us attend any inspirational gathering, we feel alive, we feel hopeful for the future, and we feel as if something within us has awakened. I call this divine consciousness. It happens when we are aligned with the Divine—or in religious terminology, the God—of our understanding.

The question that may arise is, "How can we live in this state of mind more often?" I remember the first spiritual retreat I ever attended. It was back in 2009. We were at the Kanuga Conference and Retreat Center in Hendersonville, North Carolina. It was a powerful weekend as each participant experienced the God of his or her understanding. At one point, a friend and I shared a conversation by the waterfalls. She said,

"I wish I could keep this experience every day, and not just have it here at the retreat."

This simple sentence has stayed with me since that moment. Why couldn't we keep those kinds of experiences? I believe we can. Within the depths of my being, I believe we will thrive in every aspect of our lives. Since this is a desire within my heart, it will become a reality. With that thought in mind, I present to you the four keys I have discovered to living divine consciousness.

Key 1: Be Centered in the Heart

We have discussed this in great detail previously, but let's revisit it. In every moment, we have an opportunity to choose. We either come from a place of love or from a place of fear. When we are in a place of love, we are in our hearts. When we are in a place of fear, we are in our heads. In each moment of choice that arises, all we need to do is exercise one simple activity that can take us from our heads to our hearts—breathe a deep breath. If you are a visual person, visualize a color for this breath, and see it moving from your head to your heart. If you are a feeler, then feel it moving down.

Close your eyes and take this deep breath. Give it an intention of "connecting with the heart." Simply doing this activity will bring you consciously into your heart space. Once you are in your heart, you are creating your life more consciously. When you are in your heart space, you are a "vibrational match" to that which you desire. This idea was presented in Abraham

Series Seminars, as channeled by Esther Hicks in 2010. When we are connected to our heart space, we are fully aligned with the life we desire to live.

Key 2: *Release the Care of How*

In a time and culture of control, it's not simple for us to release the "care of how." We have developed an unhealthy habit of attempting to control every experience in our lives. Some of us control in ways that are obvious. Some of us control with our emotions or obsessive thoughts. We have our desire, and we focus all of our attention on, "How will I get this?" "How will I meet that person?" "How can I possibly heal?" "How … how … how?" Our minds become so consumed by these thoughts that we miss the essential step of surrender. We unconsciously resist that which we desire because we are persistently thinking about *how* it may come to be. Many miss out on opportunities to achieve their heart's desire because the opportunities that are presented to them don't match the exact images they hold in their mind.

It's like the old parable of the man caught in the flood. He prayed desperately for God to save him. Three times, people came to help him, but he refused their help because he was waiting for God. He knew God would save him. Eventually, the man drowned, and as he stood before God, he asked, "Why did you not come and save me?" God's reply was, "I sent you help three times, and you rejected each opportunity." Had the man truly allowed himself to let go, knowing his "prayer" had been answered, he may have seen the solutions right in front of him. This happens to us more often than we realize. We pray and ask, and think about and worry about how our desire will come to be.

Many of us became that drowning man. We obsessively persist in our prayers without taking the necessary action or having true faith that our prayers will be answered. Ultimately, our actions create resistance against the flow of manifesting that which we desire.

I remember a simple desire I had while ago. I knew I had a Sunday service to prepare for, and previous experience showed me that the services that left the biggest impression on parishioners were the ones in which I shared a type of magical story about living this life in a spectacular way. I had previously spoken at this church, so I felt I needed to present something fresh. I spoke my desire, with the corresponding emotions, and I surrendered it to the Divine. I let go of how or what I wanted to experience and allowed myself to center into my heart. The next day as I was driving into town, I experienced the magic I had desired. I saw a beautiful deer standing on the side of the road. As ordinary as this experience may sound initially, it wasn't. This deer didn't seem to be frightened. He didn't leap away as most deer do when a car approaches or passes. I slowed my car to a stop and pulled over. I opened my car door and slowly walked toward the deer. The deer simply stood there and looked at me. I placed my keys on the top of my car and squatted down to be the height of the deer. I experienced a magical dance with Divine/God as the deer approached me and allowed me twelve incredible minutes as I petted him as though I were petting a friendly dog. It even allowed me to capture the moment in a few selfies! To see these images, go to www. journeyforlove.com. The images show me smiling and laughing as I captured these amazing moments as the deer sniffed my hair and placed his nose under my chin.

Isn't he beautiful? After the incredible twelve minutes passed, I returned to my car and allowed tears of joy to fall as I expressed my deep gratitude for this magical experience. The Divine had heard me and responded in kind. I now had the topic I needed, and I would be able to present an inspirational service to the church members.

While that experience was a fun one, let's take a moment to look at potential desires that may only fully integrate this key over a period of time. Sure, releasing the care of how, when having fun, can be simple. However, releasing the care of how for the desire our ego is hiding behind can be a challenge. For this, go back to the first key—every thought becomes reality. Let's look at a desire we are deeply emotionally connected to, such as finances, career, or attracting the perfect relationship. All of us have one area of our lives that is perpetually connected by the same thread of desire. We can see it when we look back on our lives. Let's look at two areas where most people struggle—relationships and finances. Regarding relationships, people want to connect to their hearts' desires of finally being with their one true soul mate. They will take many of these teachings and begin to get excited about their romance coming into full manifestation. Now let's look at finances. People connect with their deepest desire to be financially free of debt and to work in the careers of their dreams. They too connect to the excitement of the possibility of this happening.

It's within this period of early excitement that the ego creeps in. A need to feel in control begins to enter the equation. We have a few moments of excitement, and then we wonder how it will happen. Those desiring the perfect love look at every potential love affair as being "the one." Those desiring more abundance in finance fantasize about winning the lottery, winning Publishers Clearing House, or coming into money in a different way. We become obsessed with thoughts of how it will come to be, to the extent that the wondering of how turns into subtle doubt, and we develop a lack of patience with divine time. We want it on our time and in our own way. We ask, and ask, and ask in prayer over and over again. By doing this we have entered the paradigm of resisting. We find ourselves persistently asking from a place of lack. Like attracts like, so we end up unconsciously attracting a lack of what we desire rather than what we desire itself.

The key to living the life we thrive in is to release the care of *how*, and let it go. Then just *know* that your heart's desire will manifest. We do this constantly in small things that we may not have deeply emotional ties to, such as the fun example of the deer story I shared. The difference was that, with the deer, I needed only to get out of my own way and let go of focusing on the *how*.

When I have followed these keys, I have always experienced that which I desired, and I have received in ways I wouldn't have imagined. One year, my desire was for an old debt to be paid and released from my experience. I would never have imagined that it would be cleared in the way it was. (My ex took responsibility for it.) The next year, my desire was for all of the debts my spouse and I had accumulated. I'm sure anyone reading this can relate to the obsessive thoughts of lottery winnings, investments paying off, and other wild ideas. When I finally released the care of how, the solution appeared in a way I could not have predicted. One of our closest friends, who had been more like a family member than a friend, came into some money. She knew of our financial situation and, with her sudden influx of wealth, paid off all of our debts. The incredible thing was that this happened the same day I had spent the morning "blowing my breath of life" into the desire of my heart, and surrendering it. Within hours of doing that simple activity, everything I could have imagined came into existence.

This brings forward another piece of this key. When we let go of the how, and allow for the divine universe to flow in our experience, we can't miss our heart's desire coming into manifestation. In that example, I didn't need to take the inspired action of purchasing a lottery ticket. I simply needed to surrender and release the care of how.

I recently connected with a coworker who was experiencing a very challenging financial struggle. I shared two these techniques with her. I asked her to be in gratitude that her light bill was paid despite her not knowing how it would be paid. I reminded her of scripture that says, "And God said, let there be light." (Genesis 1:3 James King Version) I asked her to release the care of how, knowing that God would take care of her heart's desire. Within two days, I witnessed seven miracles, in ways neither she nor I would have ever imagined. She received over $2,000 to keep her from eviction, put her checking account back in a positive balance, and get her car out of the repair shop. This was a person who had been beyond being financially broke; she had been faced with being homeless. All it took was for her to connect to her heart's desire and then surrender it.

Key 3: Play with Possibilities Using Childlike Wonder

Remember when you were a child and you played pretend? As kids, we didn't have limitations on our possibilities because our games were all pretend. We pretended to be famous singers, star athletes, and heroes. We orchestrated the best Ken and Barbie relationships and conjured up the best teachers to teach our teddy bears or neighborhood friends. We started clubs and pretended to be anything and everything. We simply played as children.

What did you most love to pretend as a child? Did you play house? Did you play with Barbie dolls? Were you more of the outdoor child who loved playing in the woods, in the water, or climbing trees? Did you build things as a child? When you pretended to be something, what was is it? Take a moment to remember yourself as an innocent child. If your childhood was bad, then take a moment to think about where you went when you tried to pretend and retreat from your life. What made you smile?

Whatever you loved to pretend, are you doing it now in any capacity? So many of us are not. Somewhere between our childhood days and the present day, we dropped our dreams to grow up in a society that didn't really recognize the gift of who we are. We were bombarded with news and television shows that told us what to do and who to be. While attending school, we were guided to fully understand what becoming an adult was, and how we were expected to live.

The expectation was simple to understand—finish school; go to college; get a good job; buy a house; buy a car; get married; have children; and one day, when we are old, retire. In our retirement, we could live the life we had dreamed of as a child. But first, we must do the above in any order. Some of us accomplish all of the things we are "supposed" to do. Some of us complete many of them. Others complete only several. Some people may never complete any of them.

Few of us have been blessed to live a life aligned with our true desires. We were reprogrammed to do what our society needed and expected us to do. As children, we had vivid imaginations, and we had many gifts of Spirit. Many of us were very intuitive and felt everything. Others of us could see things and people that others could not see. Some of us had gifts that enabled us to manipulate experiences by simply applying our attention. All of these skills were suppressed, however, at an early age, as our well-meaning parents and teachers redirected our focus on what society expected.

The key to living divine consciousness, or "heaven on earth," is to be as children—pretend as children. Reconnect to what the heart desires, and pretend you are already doing it. Your desire may be to establish a huge business venture. It may be to be in a perfect relationship. It may be to sail around the world. Whatever it is, begin to "play pretend" with it. This may seem silly at first—*good!* Be silly with it. That silly energy and laughter will make a difference. It's not that you need to have that energy for it to become reality, but that energy will increase the speed of manifestation.

Allow yourself to play with possibilities using childlike wonder. See life experiences in a new way. Take a pause from being an adult today, and let your inner child lead the way. Take a walk outside and experience whatever you encounter with the eyes of a child.

One day I was feeling that being an adult was challenging. I was trying so hard to do well in what I had created with my business, Soul Journeys. I wanted to inspire humanity and was in my head trying to figure out what to write. I had been working on it for over an hour and was not getting anywhere.

Finally, I was guided by something within me to take a walk. I set off for the nearby park. I was plagued with constant thoughts about what I could write about … perhaps this or that. Then random thoughts began to come: "What should I make for dinner later? I wonder what time my spouse will be home. I wish I had more money so I could feel freer to do these things. Oh, I'm in nature—let me set that intention and prayer." This went on and on and on.

Suddenly I became aware of a crow making a lot of noise. (I should point out that my several animal totems love to play with me.) He just wouldn't stop all his commotion. I knew that the crow was one of my totems, so something about the commotion made me stop. I stood still, closed my eyes, and listened. I then randomly chanted "Om" three times. When I opened my eyes, the crow had stopped vocalizing, and my thoughts had calmed. I recognized the beauty that surrounded me. The sky was brilliantly blue, the trees were vibrant, and I could hear small birds and squirrels playing in the leaves. I smiled and breathed.

Then another thought came: "Oh! This is what I could write about. This would inspire people. What a cool experience this was! I love having fun like this. Oh I wish I could do this more often. Why don't I do this more often? I really need to manifest more money. What time is it? I need to get home and start dinner ..." Then I heard the crow cawing again, this time much louder than before. I stopped, closed my eyes, and laughed, realizing that I had done it again. I chanted "Om" three more times, opened my eyes, and enjoyed the silence, stillness, and beauty. As I walked further, I learned I was the only person in the entire park. There were no campers, no visitors, no park rangers—just the crow and me.

The crow was reminding me to be like a child, to let go of the to-do lists and the expectations in my thoughts and just be. He reminded me to be present in the beauty that surrounded me—to enjoy it and play in it. This is where true inspiration comes from—by purely *being*. Isn't that what we did as children? We simply played.

Key 4: Be in a Receptive State

The laws of the Universe are profound and constant. We understand the basics of the law of gravity well. When we drop our cell phone, we know without thinking that it will hit the ground. Just because I'm Becky Rector doesn't make me an exception to this law. It's the law of gravity.

We have also come to gain a great deal of understanding about the power of electricity. When we turn a light switch off, the lights go off. When we turn it on, the lights go on. We don't think about how it will happen; we *know* it will happen. We don't get lost in our thought processes: *I wonder if this will work. What if I do it wrong? How do I do it right? Am I good enough to do it?* We just know that the moment we hit the switch, the lights will go on or off. We are surprised if our expectations are not met. If, for some strange reason, we turn the light switch on and the lights don't come on, we know that something's wrong. We then make the adjustment—change the bulb, change the batteries, check the circuit breaker—and it works again.

The law of attraction, at its core, is the same. There is no exception. It always works, no matter who we are. It simply is. It's not anything new. The law of attraction has always existed. Collectively, we were simply not aware of its existence until information was brought forward in books and documentaries. It bears repeating. The law of attraction has always existed, and it is always working. If it isn't working, then something *within us* needs to be adjusted. Perhaps we are causing a blockage because we are approaching a situation from a perspective of lack. To put it another way, we set our intention around the fact that we *don't* have whatever it is we want to attract. An example of this is, "I intend to win the lottery so that I can get out of debt and stop struggling so much." The intention is focused on the *debt* and *struggling*, rather than the *abundance* that could be provided by the lottery win. Lack doesn't match prosperity; it is the antithesis of prosperity. Therefore, we unintentionally continue to attract *lack*. This can create a vicious cycle of setting an improper intention. Sometimes we do the opposite—we become upset and attempt to set another intention, this time with more emotion but still done improperly, and so we receive the same results. This can go on and on.

The adjustment we need to make here is simple: switch to a receptive state. Expect the lights to go on. Determine what you desire, and then let it go, simply expecting that it will manifest. This effort will require minimal effort on your part. One "baby step" will set the ball into motion, and the rest will happen naturally. Again, set your intention with deep emotion, let it go, and then expect that it will happen. It will happen naturally, simply just because you let it go. Before we turn the light switch on, we don't sit there waiting and hope that it will work. We just *know*, and it just *does*. As soon as you take these steps, an inspired action step will appear. You will feel called to do something, and you'll do it. As you operate in this paradigm, time will work with you. There will no longer be an experience of divine time versus our time.

Try this for a moment: Be as a child. Stand up and go to the nearest light switch. Now, turn the light switch off. Wow!

It was magical, right? Now, turn it back on. Did you see that? It happened instantly. It wasn't difficult. It was easy. You didn't have to think about it. You did it! You wanted the lights on, you took an inspired action, and you experienced the results.

Now apply that same energy to attract that which you desire. Stand up, turn the "switch" on and smile. You did it! It really is that simple. By being in this receptive state, we are open to the fact that everything will fall divinely into place. We let go of *how* it needs to happen or could happen. We simply allow it to unfold, and we take inspired action, naturally, as things unfold.

God is always working with us to align us divinely with our heart's desire. The truth is, desire is aligned with the Divine/ God. The Divine/God is simply waiting for us to say yes, and then to get out of our own way and allow for the beautiful unfolding of our dreams.

There is no need to stress over doing this the right way. Just as in meditation there is no right or wrong way to meditate. Simply meditate. There is no right way to do this; simply do it! Remember that, within you, is the way for you. You have always known it. What better time than now to make your move!

CHAPTER 5

Choosing Now

C lose your eyes and take in a deep breath. Relax and release that breath. Continue breathing like this. As you breathe in slowly and breathe out slowly, focus simply on the breath in this moment. Center yourself in this time and place. With every thought that appears, return to the breath. Simply breathe. Continue this breathing exercise for twenty breaths. Breathe in deeply, breathe out deeply, and count one. Breathe in deeply, breathe out deeply, and count two.

Welcome to this moment in time. This is the most important time of our lives—right now. So often we stay lost in the past emotional dramas of everything that has happened in our lives. Or we become consumed by hopes for, or worries over, the future. We want to be healthier, richer, and more successful. We want to have more love, more romance, more friendship, more time, more peace, more money—you add your desire. All the while, we are wasting our precious energy in this moment on wanting what we do not have in our lives or regretting what we cannot change (Tolle 1999, 49).

In this, we continue the same pattern of saying things like, "I'm going to start doing yoga." "I'm going to start investing in my future." "I'm going to stop over-committing." "I'm going to ... I'm going to ... I'm going to ..." Fast forward a year from now, or ten years, and we may find that we have done nothing to make changes and that we are still saying, "I'm going to ..."

There is so much power in taking an inspired action right now! Not tomorrow or next week—right now! When we make the first step toward that which we want, everything truly works in our favor. Oftentimes we wait for a sign from the Universe/God before taking action. The truth is the Universe/God is waiting for us.

Taking this inspired action can be as simple or as complex as we wish to make it. For instance, if we want to be healthier, it can be very simple to choose clean foods or begin a daily exercise program. If this has been an area of struggle for you, begin with small steps—replace one meal per day with a salad and take a gentle stroll outside. It's okay to ease yourself into the change, as long as you make that change. If we want to have more peace, or grow closer to the God of our understanding, then we must simply begin a meditation or prayer ritual today. If you are uncertain how to meditate, consider investing in a meditation class. If you haven't been comfortable with prayer in your life, find ways in which you are personally comfortable with talking to God The most important factor here is to do something that feels right to you. What works for one person may not work for another. Sometimes the question is bigger; for example, what about experiencing the perfect relationship? Or what about finding the perfect job? What actions can we take to bring about more money or love? The answer to these questions may be as simple as allowing whatever inspired action shows up for that day to transpire. This could come as a nudge to answer an ad in the paper or a sudden urge to have lunch at the local café where you've seen that cute cashier. The point is to take time each day to visualize and discover our heart's desire. Once we know our desire, we can do one small thing every day that will take us toward that dream, whatever that dream may be.

We are connected to the God of our understanding through our hearts. This is where God speaks to us. When we meditate and connect to our hearts, we are listening to God. I have shared this before; a desire within our heart wouldn't be there if there wasn't divinely orchestrated support available to us. In aligning with our heart's desire, we are aligning with God. We are living the truth of who we really are, whether our desire is as simple as living a healthier lifestyle, or as expansive as taking a trip across the world, or as complex as our jobs, relationships, or relocation of our homes. By aligning with our hearts we are no longer aligning with what others say is best for us; we are aligning with what we know to be best for us.

CHAPTER 6

*Awareness of Where We
Focus Our Energy*

Whatever we focus our energy on is what we will continue to create or draw into our lives. We are all energetic beings. This has been proven by quantum physics and is discussed in books such as *Vibrational Medicine* by Richard Gerber, MD. Let us dig deeper into this understanding.

Creating Reality

For most of our lives we have been unconscious to the universal laws that affect us. Many of us have learned in recent years about the famous law of attraction. Rather than explaining how this law works, I'd like to dig into it deeper. For a more basic understanding of the law of attraction you can find many books on the subject, such as *Law of Attraction: The Basics of the Teachings of Abraham* by Ester and Jerry Hicks, and *The Secret* by Rhonda Byrne. Many wonderful writers communicate this subject beautifully.

You should first understand that absolutely every moment of our lives, with absolutely every thought we have, we are creating our realities through the law of attraction. There is not an experience we have that does not originate from our own divine minds. Let's look at the unconscious creating modality.

When I was a child, I grew up watching Lifetime movies and daytime drama soaps such as *Days of Our Lives*. I remember how frightened I was when Carly was buried alive on *Days of Our Lives*. I recall how excited I was when she was found. I remember poor Bo grieving when he knew Hope had died. Watching movies, I cried at the devastation of people who were grieving over losses. Many of the Lifetime movies I watched contained themes of pain and loss. I can remember a story about of a group of messed-up teens who killed their parents. I can recall movies about missing children, and parents grieving the loss of children killed either by accident or at the hands of others. I remember so many movies about people who were murdered. The list goes on. These were high-drama movies that absolutely created great compassion because of how sad they were. I felt empathy for the characters. This level of "drama" continued on the news, which my mom and dad watched constantly. I also recall watching *Unsolved Mysteries* with my grandma and grandpa. This show, my grandma's favorite, presented mysteries about unsolved crimes, unexplained historical events, and paranormal events. Every Wednesday night we would watch it together. This show was very scary, but

I couldn't resist watching every week with her. This was all a part of my upbringing, and the culture in my little Midwestern town.

I now understand that, as I watched those real and fictionalized events on TV, thoughts were being created within me that added to my existing fears. I had fears of dying, fears of being kidnapped, fears of fears of fears. Even before my birth, my mom, bless her heart, had always had fears upon fears. She grew up having many abusive and tragic things happen in her life. For her, watching the TV dramas provided a sense of not feeling so alone in the world. On some level she could relate to the pain she saw on the screen.

The first manifestation of these fears in my awareness came when a local teen was kidnapped at the Venture Department Store in my small town. Looking back now, I wonder if this was the Universe's way of offering me a heads-up of what I was unconsciously creating. The evidence would point me to that conclusion when, one Wednesday evening as I joined my grandma to watch *Unsolved Mysteries*, I was faced with the recent happening in our little town. The kidnapping had made my town famous on *Unsolved Mysteries*. I thought about my deep connection to this show and wondered if I had somehow, unconsciously, contributed to this event in some way. Later it was found—or at least suspected—that the victim had been picked up by either devil worshipers, as some in the town believed, or she had been taken to Florida and sold into slavery, as others believed. Either way, my fears were manifesting into reality, and it was all a little too close to home.

What did I know at that age? I was only eight. I had no understanding of how thoughts created reality. At age nine, it struck home. It was August 23, 1987. My mom, dad, younger sister, and I had gone out to the American Legion. This was a normal thing to do on the weekends. Dad was commander in chief, and he had created the facility to be a family sort of place. We had a playground out back and a game room where kids could play. My older brother, Tim, who was seventeen, was at a going-away party for a friend who would soon join the service. That night remains crystal clear in my memory, even now. My sister and I had so much fun that night with Mom and Dad. Mom was even chasing us in the parking lot, playing tag with Patty and me. I remember, as we were driving home, thinking, "This has been the best day of my life. I have had so much fun—more fun than ever." These words have haunted me for many years.

Patty and I had gone to bed when I heard Mom getting upset in the living room. Dad was angry. Mom was worried. Tim was late for curfew. Mom said he was never late. Dad reminded her he had been late "that one night." Mom reminded him it was because he got lost in St. Louis. Mom called the friend's house where Tim had gone for the party. They told Mom that Tim had left hours before her call. Mom then called the local authorities. The authorities said there had been a wreck off Highway Z, but Tim hadn't been involved. In the small town where I lived, everyone knew everyone. Mom then got in her car and went to look for Tim. I sat on the sofa, shaking. I was afraid. I felt as if I was watching an episode of *Unsolved Mysteries* unfold in my home. Dad was not worried; he was more aggravated than anything else.

It must have been an hour later when I looked out the window to see Mom getting out of a police car. She walked into our house, went upstairs and woke my sister up, and then sat us all down with dad. She looked into my father's eyes. Through her tears, Mom said, "Our son is gone." My immediate thoughts were, *He's been kidnapped! Where is he? We need to go find him!* Then dad asked what she meant, and Mom said it again, "Our son is gone." She then asked Dad if he wanted to go to see Tim that night—in the morgue. In that moment, I realized my brother was dead. I went with my parents to the morgue to see him. I remember the thought that came to my mind upon seeing him: *He was beat up.* They said it was a car wreck. We later learned that he had been murdered.

When tragedy hits, there are many ways a person's psyche tries to cope. Marriages end, families rip apart, kids go into dark places. People die. My family grieved in what I can only describe by using the word *interestingly.* I did what I unconsciously knew to do. I stepped into my brother's shoes to take care of my sister and make sure Mom and Dad would be okay. I went from being a nine-year-old girl to taking on the role and responsibilities of someone closer to nineteen years old.

As sad as that story is, today I am grateful for the incredible teachings it has offered me along the way. Often I have been asked, "If it's true that we create our own reality, why and how is tragedy created?" No one chooses tragedy, right? How do bad things happen to good or young people? My answer is this:

fear creates reality too. What is the cure for this? *Love!* I know now that my brother is in an amazing place. It is my love for him that has helped me to overcome the fears brought on by his death.

I share this part of my life here simply to show the evidence of unconscious creating. Now, did I create my brother's death? There is no way to know for certain. What I know is that I created the experience of having a tragedy in my life. It's what I had focused on the most, albeit unconsciously. From this experience, I have also learned to recognize my thoughts and what I focus my attention upon. I now filter what I watch on the television, and I have become more aware of the conversations I engage in. Time and time again, when I look back, I see how what I focused my energy on created the reality in which I was living.

Creating Consciously

Flash forward to the fall of 2010 when I visited the Carolinas for the first time. I was attending a conference for the ministry through which I had been ordained. I had the most amazing experience with that group, and I recall the first time I visited the waterfalls at Dupont State Forest—Triple Falls and Hooker Falls. It was a breathtaking experience. I went back to that place before the end of that powerful conference to meditate and simply enjoy the beauty. In my final moments there, I took a deep breath and said, "God, I would love to live somewhere like this and have the ability to come here every day." I then got back into my car and headed home to Florida.

So, my heart's desire was to live in a place as beautiful as that spot in Dupont State Forest, and that desire continued to build from there. I wasn't aware of what was happening yet, but I continued to create. With little more consciousness than a child possesses, I kept creating. In the year to follow, I began envisioning what it would be like to live my life doing my ministry a hundred percent of the time. What would it look like to let go of my corporate job and just teach, heal, and minister about love? In my meditations, I would affirm gratitude for these things. In conversations with my close, like-minded friends, I would discuss how great it would be to teach people how to meditate and other things of that nature.

In the spring of 2011, I made an appointment to speak with my teacher, Rev. Bob, to discuss my dissertation for my doctorate of divinity in metaphysics and spirituality. I shared with him my ideas, and then the conversation took an unexpected turn. He said he wasn't sure if it was the right time, but he wanted to meet with me to discuss the possibility of training me to take over the operations of the Seraphim Center. This was his spiritual center, the one he had created thirteen years prior to our conversation. It was his love. He shared that he wished to retire and travel more with his wife. He continued on to say that, in the event of his passing, he would like to pass the center to me. He assigned me the task of thinking about this, and he asked me to let him know my decision. It took all of five minutes to formulate my answer: yes. I could imagine saying nothing else.

When we began the training, instead of teaching me operations, Rev. Bob passed on his many years of profound wisdom, which he had gained throughout his spiritual and metaphysical journey. I looked forward to the few hours I spent with him every week. In late August 2011, Rev. Bob planned our trip to Maine, where I was to graduate and confer my vows for my doctorate degree. I had, by this time, been voted in as a board member of the Seraphim Center, and I was to take the position of president of the board if anything were to happen to Rev. Bob.

One week before my graduation, my teacher, Rev. Bob, fell ill and was hospitalized. We mutually agreed that I needed to continue with my plans to travel to Maine and complete my graduation. Rev. Bob's colleague and dear friend would confer my vows. When I returned to Florida, I found that his illness had worsened. By January 1, 2012, I was running the Seraphim Center full time. I surrendered my sales and cleaning careers and dedicated my life a hundred percent to the ministry.

The Center truly thrived. I was surprised by this, since the spiritual leader had passed on, but membership in the Center continued to grow in numbers. We grew so much that we outgrew our meeting location and began the process of purchasing a permanent home for the Center—a dream Rev. Bob would love to have fulfilled. I had so much fun throughout my journey with the Center. I could teach every Sunday morning or pull in amazing and powerful speakers to present. We offered book groups, meditation groups, and more. I learned the daily operations through trial-by-fire, and spent most of my time at the Center.

I continued to connect to my heart's desire. I visualized more things that made me feel joy inside. I traveled to South Carolina to receive training by a new teacher. Logically, I didn't understand this, but on every trip, the moment I crossed the state line into South Carolina, I felt myself able to breathe again. I envisioned what it would be like to have opportunities to visit more and more often. I even remember planting my feet on the ground and saying, "God, I would love to be able to live in a place like this."

Do you remember the song from the children's movie, *The Incredible Mr. Limpet*? The song is, "Be Careful What You Wish For." As I mentioned in the introduction of this book, on December 21, 2012, I was offered a job in the Carolinas that I simply didn't want to refuse. It was perfect. It aligned with all of my spiritual aspirations and my fascination with technology and leadership. I could also continue leading the Seraphim Center from my new home in the Carolinas. This new job opportunity was truly a blessing, especially in a financial sense. From the moment I took on the Seraphim Center, my annual salary went from $40,000 a year to $6,000 a year. No, that is not a typo—I mean $6,000. I believed that I could survive this financial crisis through complete faith and love.

After I returned to Florida and shared this great news with my partner, my journey toward my truest heart's desire really began. I knew deep within that I wanted to be living in the

Carolinas. I didn't really know why. The job offer was more of a carrot than the end goal, but it was leading me to where my heart desired to be.

Here is where the understanding of the heart's desire truly starts. If I compared my experience at the Seraphim Center to my past experience of unconsciously creating through fear, I could see a similarity to the experience of the kidnapping of the young girl in my hometown. Let me explain. This job offer was the Universe's way of giving me a heads-up of what was about to come. Perhaps this job was manifested to see how connected to my desire I wished to be. Sure, during any moment, faced with the challenges with the Seraphim Center, I could have run back to the comforts of my prosperous career in corporate America. Instead, I continued to move forward, learning the grace required to truly live in the flow of life.

My choice to move led to the closing of many doors in my Florida life. I went through the painful experience of ending of an eleven-year relationship. Friends I thought would be there for me, as I had been for them, didn't seem ready or willing to offer me any support, not even a sofa to sleep on for a few days. Interestingly, the person who was there for me most was my ex. There were so many days of sadness, grief, and uncertainty. I wondered if I had made the right decision. There were so many times I thought that, perhaps, I should just stay and say no to the job. Maybe it would be best to just continue on as I had been doing. However, when I went within, to tune into my heart, my heart danced for joy at the very thought of being in the Carolinas. So I prayed for grace. Every moment of every day, I prayed for grace.

On the day of my departure, I realized the magnitude of what I was leaving behind. In essence I was leaving the life I had spent years building. I was leaving to my ex the home I had invested so much in and owned. I was leaving my pets behind. I was leaving everything I knew behind, including the cleaning company I had founded, and I was starting from scratch. I had absolutely no money in savings. I had no credit cards. I truly had only ten dollars in my bank account. I didn't even know how I would make it to Atlanta for training. To put it simply, all I had was faith. As I began my trip, I stopped to say farewell to my dear friend who had been a loving provider of support throughout my journey. She gave me a farewell card that contained three gas cards for Shell stations. That got me to the training and then to Brevard, North Carolina.

Many have asked why I would leave the eleven-year relationship, the home, and the cleaning company I had invested years of my life in. The answer is simple—it was the most loving thing to do. Those things were not in alignment with my heart's desire, and if I stayed they would have eventually fallen away regardless of my choices. Maintaining a healthy friendship with my ex meant a great deal to me then, and it still does now. If I hadn't surrendered the relationship, we might both have ended up with many regrets.

I arrived in the Carolinas to discover that my new bosses had paid the first and last months' rent on a sweet cottage for me. They had used my first paycheck to get me settled and ready for work. While we waited for the cottage to be made move-in ready, they welcomed me into their home. I had brought no furniture, no dishes—nothing but my clothes, books, and some sentimental belongings. I truly had left everything to my ex. I planned to buy a blow-up air mattress with my first paycheck, and I simply didn't think much about it. I didn't worry, and I didn't stress. I just focused on being present in my life. Two days before moving into my cottage, my mom called to share the news that she had won her settlement with a medical law suit, and she was mailing me a check for $11,000 to purchase whatever furniture I needed.

In less than two weeks after I left Florida, I was living a life of heaven on earth. Guess what? It got even better! While working one day at the office, my bosses' son came by. He said that he was on his way to go swimming at—wait for it … are you sitting down?—Hooker and Triple waterfalls! Without realizing it, I now lived five minutes from the very place I had first planted the seed of my heart's desire in 2010! While meditating at this magical place in 2010, I had connected to a deep heart's desire and planted a seed thought. I recall saying, "I wish I was able to be here every day, if only I could." You can imagine my overwhelming joy to realize how close I had landed to my dream spot! Then, to add to this, even though I thought it couldn't get any better, it did! While sitting on my porch, I realized that my view was exactly what I had envisioned when leading others in guided meditations for the past few years. The meditation went like this:

> Imagine you are walking on a beautiful path in nature. It's a perfect and beautiful day. You come upon a white fence with a white gate. As you walk in, there is a perfectly still lake with a white bridge over it, and a white pavilion next to the lake with geese floating in the water.

This was now my view! As I took that all in I said, "God, how can it get any better than this?" And then it did.

Today, I am happily married to my soul mate and love of my life. We live in the most amazing home surrounded by a state park with an amazing mountain view. My spouse is everything that my heart ever desired and more. Even the littlest things in my life bring joy. My life is amazing, and it keeps getting better. I launched my own ministry, Soul Journeys, LLC, which offers one-day workshops dedicated to uplifting and inspiring humanity. I am back in a great job with great pay and benefits, and I'm still doing the work of my heart. I am now clearly aware of how I created all of this consciously.

I share all of this because the best evidence I can provide is my own personal experience. At the end of my book, I will introduce four other individuals I have studied and worked with, and who have seen the exact same results.

So, I pose the question again—what is your heart's desire? The simple answer is this: it is that which you most want in your life. To help you figure out what it is, ask yourself this question, "If I had a million dollars, what would I do?" If you won the lottery, if you had better health, if you had a better relationship … if … if … what would you do? The answer you receive when you ask that question is most likely aligned with your heart's desire.

The truth I have learned is this: humanity is waiting for us to step into our truest desire. Once we do, not only will we be thriving, but humanity will thrive. That includes your spouse, your kids, your job, your health, your finances, and every part of your life. What would this world be like had Wayne Dyer said, "Well, yes, but I have a wife and kids. I can't quit my job and take my book and message on the road" Or had Melissa Etheridge said, "Thanks for offering to record my music, but I've got this girlfriend, this house, and these bills. I can't just drop all that and go on the road." What if Tony Robbins had said, "Well, that's nice that you want me to come speak and motivate, but who would listen to me?" I can go on and on with a list of those who have inspired me. I can't imagine what my world would be like if they had said no to their heart's desire because of an illusion created by fear.

CHAPTER 7

Our Divine Breath of Life

We have this incredible gift of breath and words. As a Reiki master, I have learned that, when I use my breath, especially with sound, the power of the energy healing is intensified.

The difference, which can be felt, comes with the intensity of our breath. I use the phrase "breathe your breath of life" to symbolize adding more power to our heart's desire. When we add power to our heart's desire, we also remove any residual fear or attachment.

Many religions and spiritual paths discuss the importance of breath. In the Christian teachings, we believe that we are made in the likeness and image of God. Building from that, we have a powerful teaching in the book of Genesis in the form of God breathing the breath of life into Adam. In the book of John it is taught that "In the beginning was the word, and the word was with God, and the word was God" (John 1:1 NKJV). Here, "the word" represents "the breath."

The creation story gives us powerful messages about the

creative force within us. We are told that we are made in the image and likeness of God. We understand that God breathed his breath of life to create life. We are also taught that, "In the beginning was the Word, and the Word was with God, and the Word was God" (John 1:1 King James Version). In this reference, when we have combined the breath of life with the spoken word, we have created as God did. We are taught that if we have the faith of a mustard seed, we can truly move mountains.

When we put this all together, we have a powerful formula for creating our heart's desire and making it manifest. When we realize that we are created in the image of God, that we have the divine breath of life within us, and that our faith can help to remove all obstacles on our path to living our heart's desire, we have the power to make it manifest. Emma Curtis Hopkins (the teacher of teachers, who taught Myrtle and Charles Fillmore of Unity Churches) described this in great detail in her book, *The Radiant I Am*, in which she affirms her ministry: "I think this, I write this, I speak this, I live this" (Hopkins 2007, 109). In the scripture, we learn: "And all things you ask in prayer, believing, you will receive" (Matthew 21:22 New American Standard Bible).

So, how do we breathe our breath of life? We do this by being aware of our words. We do this when we engage in conversations with friends, family members, and coworkers, and even when we talk to ourselves or voice our prayers and affirmations during meditation. Speaking is our "breath of life." We breathe or speak our breath of life all the time. Often our choice of words is unconscious, and our words can have a negative or positive effect. We may engage in gossip with others. We may get caught up in venting about the life we are living, which isn't aligned with our dreams. We may pray from a place of lack and fear. We may continue to wish and pray, over and over, for that which we don't have. That is what we are breathing our precious breath of life into.

Imagine the power of our word consciously being used to create that which we wish to experience, rather than that which we do not. It's very much like the magical word *abracadabra*. When we begin to consciously breathe our breath of life into that which we want, we move mountains. Each time I have done the breath of life meditation, the exercise has provided what I consider instant manifested results. A reminder: when you engage in this activity, you should be passionately connected to the words being spoken. The more emotion you muster, the better the results.

Breath of Life Meditation

Close your eyes and take in a long and deep breath. Gently release that breath with love. Take in another deep and fully conscious breath. Breathe it out slowly. Continue breathing in and breathing out, feeling the power of your breath.

Now focus your awareness on the top of your head. Take in a deep breath. As you breathe out, blow with sound toward the top of your head. Feel the energy there. Now focus your awareness on your shoulders. Take in a deep breath, and with a loud breath out, breathe to your shoulders. Now, with awareness, breathe energy to your lower back, and then your abdomen, and then down your legs.

Continue breathing your powerful breath. Now imagine you are sitting in a theater watching yourself on the big screen, living your heart's desire. See all the characters in this movie. See the background, and see your star actor or actress. Genuinely watch this movie for a few moments.

Now take in a deep breath, and with all of your might, blow your breath of life into this image. See, feel, and hear this breath touching the screen, and see it as a wind blowing. Affirm, "With the faith of a mustard seed, I activate my divine creative force and affirm my heart's desire as good."

Now smile with gratitude as you breathe gently and slowly, bringing awareness back to your body. When you are ready, open your eyes and step fully into the life of your heart's desire.

The Breath of Life and Change

When we truly breathe our breath of life into our heart's desire, our lives shift in profound and unexpected ways. There is nothing to analyze or push for. By pushing or attempting to control any of the shifts, you will only slow the process down and create unnecessary struggle.

Once we breathe into our hearts, we need only to go with the flow. Our cardiovascular systems can act as beautiful symbols to remind us of the dynamic flow of life. As we breathe into our hearts, our hearts pump, and the blood flows to all of our vital organs. This is what continues to bring the flow of life force into our physical beings. Our heart's desires are aligned with this system.

Once we connect to our heart's desire, we must ensure that we fully and consciously think, speak, and write about that which we desire. When thoughts or conversations come up that are not in alignment with our heart's desire, we can simply choose a different thought or feeling or redirect the conversation. There is no need for any struggle. Struggle is part of the ego, which is driven by fear. Simply focusing our energy on what we want is breathing our breath of life.

I encourage you to try the following activity, using whatever is within your heart. First, write your heart's desire down on paper, several times if necessary, so it is clear and precise. Here are some examples:

- My heart's desire is to fully connect to the divine being I am and experience all the prosperity and wealth I have ever desired.
- My heart's desire is to fully connect to the beautiful person I am, and be completely aligned with my perfect loving partner.
- My heart's desire is to be divinely whole in a body that feels healthy in every way.

Formulate whatever you want in a powerful sentence that aligns with your heart. You will know that it aligns when, after you have written it, your heart beats a little louder with excitement and joy.

Now that you have written it, say it out loud one time, and then close your eyes for a moment. Allow yourself to visualize living this experience. Feel the emotions of truly being in this experience. Now open your eyes and, with all of those emotions, loudly say your statement. Say it as loud as you can. At the end of this statement, breathe out the loudest breath you can. This final step is greatly important. Surrender it now to the Divine/God. Let it go completely, and go back to whatever your day holds. If a thought shows up about it, simply smile and allow your heart to feel excited.

Go back and complete the breath of life meditation described above. Then make a commitment or vow to yourself, using your powerful breath and words to serve your heart. Walk away from or change conversations that are not in alignment with your heart. When fear shows up, allow it to be your reminder to focus on your heart's desire. This one technique can truly change the world. Why make such a bold statement? I have come to deeply understand Gandhi's words: "to see the change you want to see, be the change." As I change my breath and words, my life experience changes.

Absolutely everything outside of us is but a mirror of what is within us. When we see our lives from that perspective, we become empowered to "be the change." This process begins with shifting our paradigms.

CHAPTER 8

Shifting Paradigms

While it may be simple to bring awareness to where we focus our energy, as it's found in the themes that run our thoughts and many of our conversations, it can be much more difficult to shift our paradigms. Shifting paradigms can also create a great deal of fear in many of us because it means that change is inevitable. Despite this fear, a shift in paradigms is often necessary to release old ways of doing and begin to make room for the new life we wish to live.

To shift paradigms, we must first identify our current paradigm. Often, we discover that we have been placing our focus on either something we are resisting against or something we are persisting toward. You may have heard the saying, "what we resist will persist." To begin the necessary shift, I suggest that we look at this saying in reverse. By doing so, we find the key that leads to many blockages of the manifestation of our heart's desire.

What Persists, Resists

Whatever we persistently focus on resists coming into our experience. I will tell you about my own personal example of this phenomenon. It involves something I have persistently focused on for my entire adult life—my finances and career. As I reflect back on my life and see this, I find it humorous now. It wasn't at the time, but I have come so far since then.

I was introduced to the concept of the law of attraction when I watched the documentary, *The Secret*, by Rhonda Byrne in 2008. Completely excited to the core of my being, I began a daily practice of meditation and intention. I convinced my partner to participate with me in many activities outlined in that documentary. In my meditation, I wrote out what I was grateful for, including things I wanted to experience that hadn't manifested yet. I wrote things like "a happier relationship," "a promotion at work," "more income," "winning the lottery," and "my mom to miraculously get better." This last one was a big one for me.

The year 2008 was one of the most challenging years in my adult life. At the beginning of that year, my mom underwent open-heart surgery. The surgery appeared to have been a success; however, three days after the procedure, it was discovered that she had a severe staph infection. The infection was so bad and progressive that it destroyed her sternum. She underwent emergency surgery, and everything went downhill from there. She was in and out of the surgical intensive care unit. I became consumed with making my sales job appointments in Daytona

Beach, where my parents lived. My career proved to be very convenient for that time in my life, as it offered flexibility in both location and scheduling. I worked hour upon hour to create opportunities in Daytona so I could be there to help Dad while Mom was in the hospital. Besides the numerous hours I spent working, I also did all I could to balance my relationship and home life, where we had a collection of "kids"—dogs, cats, birds, and other dependents. My days ran together as we watched my mom slowly drifting away. At one point, the doctors said there truly was nothing else they could do. It was up to my mom.

My siblings and I were blessed with amazing parents, and Mom was our number-one cheerleader. She was always proud of us kids and my dad and spoke highly of us. My dad and I drew closer than ever that year as we did all we could to keep mom alive. We learned the valuable lesson of never leaving a loved one in the hospital alone. Someone should be there every day.

In the midst of all of this, I learned about the law of attraction, and I began my daily meditation practice. What is most clear now, as I look back, is *where* I had been focusing most of my energy. I had released any ideas of a miraculous healing for my mom. I loved her so, but I knew that it would be a matter of time. So when I added to my meditation list "my mom to have a miraculous healing" I put it in there for the sake of loving her. I invested little energy into it. I remember crying after I wrote it as I shook my head in grief; I fully expected to lose her.

I placed a great deal of energy into the intentions surrounding "increased finances and career." I remember writing an amount for a lottery win on a deposit slip and doing a ritual burial of it. I played a game with my partner: every time we walked to the mailbox we would jump for joy at the bills coming in, pretending each one was a check for double the amount of the debt. I created visualizations. Every day I would put energy into getting a raise, winning the lottery, being promoted, and succeeding. I enjoyed focusing on all of this, as it was a distraction from the stress and sadness in my life. I persistently focused all of my energy on manifesting the lottery win and financial increase.

By the year's end, here is what I had manifested. My relationship grew stronger. My partner and I had opened a commercial cleaning company, and we were getting checks in the mail. I was happier and had created a daily meditation practice. Miraculously and unexpectedly, my mom came out of it. After eleven months in surgical ICU, she took a turn for the better. She is still with us today, and her heart is in great shape.

Virtually everything I had written and intended did become manifest—except for the increase in finances and the lottery win. Yes, we were getting checks in the mail from our cleaning company, but my sales job was shifting in a negative way. Rather than giving me a salary increase, the company changed the sales department payment plan from salary plus commission to commission only. I experienced a significant decrease in pay. And the lottery win? Not even a fifty-dollar gain in the year.

Why was this? How is it that everything else became manifest—even the one I truly didn't expect to see—but not the ones I had been most focused on? I discovered that *where* I focused my energy was the key.

When we persistently focus on the desire of obtaining something, we are coming from a place of lack—a place of not having it. This was the stance I had taken with my intentions of winning the lottery and gaining an increase in finances. But I couldn't let go of this intention the way I could with the others. With all the other intentions, I could do the step that is most important in the law of attraction equation: I could let go of them. This was especially true with my mom's healing. Because I didn't expect to the intention to work with life, sickness, and death, I had completely let it go. Yet, that manifested in the strongest way.

Throughout that entire year, my daily thoughts and emotions were focused on that increase in my finances and a lottery win. I thought about what I could do if I won the lottery. I thought about paying off my mom's growing medical bills so my dad could be at ease. I thought about paying off my home and paying off Mom and Dad's home. I thought about going back to school to pursue that which I had always wanted to do. I wanted to teach in some capacity. I focused all of my energy there in every way. Yet, it didn't come to pass.

Look at your life today. Where are you focusing your energy? For some, it's manifesting that perfect relationship, finding a true soul mate. For others, it's to heal from pain or sickness. For many, it's increased wealth. How often do we spend our daily energy on wanting and affirming those desires to become manifest? I imagine most readers will agree that the majority of their time is focused on wanting what they do not have in their lives.

Now that we have an awareness of this, there is a simple process we can do to release what we are persistently focusing on. This process will enable our intentions to finally become manifest in our lives. Honestly, it takes only two words to experience this release. Ready, get set, *let go!*

I realize this has been said before, but truly, *let it go!* Now, let's fast forward from 2008 to 2015. I still focused on my desire to manifest more financial stability. I had done affirmations and tried letting the intention go. I sampled different hypnotic work and attended prosperity classes. I didn't allow others to see what I was persistently focusing on. I just continued to know I could manifest that which I desired. I saw a thread in 2014. What people persistently focused on seemed to that which was consistently *not* manifesting for them in their lives. I counseled women who desired to meet that love of their life. I worked with people who were in tremendous pain or who were very sick. Seeing the thread, I taught them to focus the same energy they directed toward the areas where they were thriving and place that energy on whatever they sought to attract into their life. I emphasized that they needed to focus on the end result, and not the sense of lack in their lives because this would only attract more lack.

On average, we thrive in at least one—and often two—areas in our lives. I worked with one woman who always thrived in the world of finance and career, but lacked in achieving any fulfilling relationships. I counseled her to expect the fulfilling relationships with the same energy she expected finance. In her case, she did not direct any energy or specific thoughts toward her finances. She just always *knew* that she would be fine financially, and she lived accordingly. She knew this with the same type of knowing we experience when we flip a light switch and know the lights will go on.

After seeing this thread, I came to a point of complete surrender. Driving to work one morning, and talking to God on my way, I said, with a great deal of emotion, "I give up. It is too hard for me to simply ask to have my bills paid off so I can comfortably purchase the product I need for my hair or buy my spouse a gift without stressing out over my dwindling account. I'm done! I'm done with trying. I surrender it all." I loudly continued, "I want to manifest this reality so much, and with the faith like that of a mustard seed, which has the power to move mountains, I have absolute faith in this happening now!" *And I let it go completely!* That was the first morning I released any thoughts about it. I was completely in the present throughout my day—no thoughts about finances. I was grateful for my job, very grateful for my amazing marriage, and just enjoyed being in the moment.

Halfway through the day, my spouse tried to call and text me. When I finally called back I heard this, "Baby, remember I told you about our family member who used to purchase so many lottery tickets? I was so concerned that she might fall into that again?" I said, "Yes, of course. Is everything okay?"

My spouse responded, "Well, I was right. She has been, and we no longer have anything to worry about." Confused I asked for clarification. "She just won the lottery—in a large way—and is paying off all of our existing bills!" Instantly I thought, *Oh, my God! It worked!*

I had surrendered. I had given up. I had released my intention, and it had manifested in a way that I would have never expected. This experience taught me a vital lesson: wasting this divine, precious gift of connecting with my heart's desire, blowing my breath of life into it, and allowing inspired action to guide me with wanting myself to experience a lottery win had been preventing me from experiencing the miraculous unfolding of a loving "earth angel" gifting my spouse and I with a portion of her unexpected wealth. I didn't win the lottery, a visualization I had oftentimes wasted my imagination on. I simply became open and receptive to "God's plan" by getting out of the way. I had let go, and to this day I still find myself humbled with tears of deep gratitude.

Since that moment, I have finally lived the life I have always had in my mind to live. I was promoted at my job. I am making more of a salary than I had requested, and I am thriving in my finances. My spouse is supportive and takes care of me, as I continue to excel and succeed in my career. I don't share this in the energy of bragging; rather, I share this to show we can truly live our lives while thriving in every way. It truly keeps getting better and better.

Shift Happens

Whatever exists in our lives that doesn't match the desires of our hearts will become challenging. Things that may not have bothered us before will bother us now. Relationships can become challenging, whether we see this in our jobs, our homes, the general environment, or anywhere else we hold a connection. This is all helping us shift our paradigm. It can be difficult to understand what or why this upheaval is happening. Fear can also show up, and it will slow down the process of manifestation. By examining the heart's desires of the five people whose case studies I offer later in this book, we will see this process a little more clearly.

It is amazing how everything that is connected to our heart's desires falls into place. The Universe lines up everything and everyone perfectly into place. When we thrive, humanity thrives, which is what the Universe ultimately wants for us. This is why the Universe will appear to bend to help us make our heart's desires a reality. In the case study of Cathy, for example, we will see a wonderful example of universal alignment and how our thriving leads to humanity's thriving. She officially opened her store and formed partnerships with local farmers and other natural food stores in local communities within three short months from the day of the Living Your Heart's Desire Workshop. Every time there seemed to be a little bump in the road, immediately support would appear. By spring of 2014, All Things Herbal celebrated a grand opening.

We can't experience this level of success if we are focusing our energy on simply having "a job." If we aren't willing to take a leap of faith and quit that "other job" or go part time in order to pursue our true passion, then remaining at the job will become more and more challenging. Relationships with coworkers and managers may become difficult and strained. It may even appear that, suddenly, things just don't seem to go right. It may get more and more intense until we finally give in and go with the flow, or have a nervous breakdown and get fired. That's exactly what occurred for Cathy. Things became difficult for her at work. It came to a head when she was written up by the employer for taking time to fill the bird feeders outside the workplace. To Cathy this did not appear to be an ordinary job performance issue; it appeared irrational, and was just another indication it was time to leave.

When we take a moment to step away from the drama, we see exactly why certain things have been occurring. If our dream is to own an organic health food store, and we are working in a real estate job, that is not a match. One of the two must go. If we hope to have a relationship with specific characteristics and these don't match our current relationship, then either we let go of that desire or things in that relationship will change. Does this mean we must lose the job or that our relationship will end? It may or it may not. What will happen is that the job or relationship will change. In matters of the heart, the relationship may move to a new level. Challenges may appear on both sides offering opportunities to grow. In matters of the job, a new position may open that provides more time and freedom for what the heart desires.

The truth is *things will change*. They will have to. We have all heard stories about people who win millions in the lottery only to end up destitute. We wonder why this happens. It's simple— these people continued to function from a place of lack. They rushed out to buy all the things they thought would make them feel better or that would fill some void within them, only to discover that the hole was still there, and they were back to square one with nothing to show for their blessing but a bunch of "stuff." In order to live the life we believe we would love to live we need to allow the paradigms to shift for us. We need to shift from the perspective of "lack" to one of "abundance." This is important because it is the only way we can fully align our lives with the new paradigm—the one that will allow our desire to unfold. If our consciousness is still operating from the level of lack, our lives will always shift to match that mindset. When we allow ourselves to shift to feeling, seeing, thinking, and experiencing our lives as a more prosperous, and seeing ourselves as giving persons, we will match the paradigm that includes a life of wealth and abundance. This is where a true paradigm shift occurs. My own personal experience with shifting paradigms came after I prayed daily for grace.

It all goes back to when I took a leap of faith in 2012 and jumped from one paradigm to the next. It was a period of significant growth in my life. My desires no longer matched my current relationship. In Florida, I was the people pleaser and working from the moment I woke up to the moment I went to sleep, with only five hours, on average, of sleep per night. In that paradigm, I was cleaning for my own business—commercial properties, postconstruction properties, and apartments when they turned over. Besides this, I was running a church and trying to fit in time to counsel and heal others. All the while I was in a relationship in which we both felt that we were approaching a point when we would both have to choose: stay together or part ways. Personally, I knew I would need to either give up what was within my heart or give up the relationship. In this relationship, I had always had to give up who I really was so I could be what my partner needed and wanted me to be. This is an error so many of us make.

At this point in my life, there was not a single part of my heart's desire within my paradigm. My heart's desire was to be in the Carolinas. My desire was to live there and to do what I most loved to do, which is to teach, heal, and write. I also desired that my partner would support all of my endeavors, and I would not have to do any type of work that didn't fit my desires. My reality was a stark contrast to my heart's desire. I found myself as part owner of a commercial cleaning company for which I also worked as a laborer. My days were filled. I would work at Seraphim Center from nine in the morning to around seven in the evening, and sometimes later. Then I would rush from job site to job site to clean toilets, vacuum, dust, mop, and whatever else was necessary. When all of that was done, I would go home and finally go to sleep at around two in the morning, just to get up and do it all over again. Even the weekends were not my own. I often worked on either Saturday or Sunday for the cleaning company. And I also ran services at the Seraphim Center, which were occasionally followed by classes that I had to teach. I found it nearly impossible to leave the church any time before half past two in the afternoon. My partner had absolutely no desire to even vacation with me in the Carolinas, and the concept of moving was not an option for her. Our desires in life were creating more and more of a valley between us. Both of our paradigms had to change. My partner desired to work hard, make a lot of money to pay the bills, and to play more. She wanted to go mudding, fishing, and jet skiing. She wanted to take vacations with her siblings rather than with me. These were her desires and, as fun as all of that sounded, I didn't share in those desires.

My paradigm had to shift if I was to thrive in the life my heart so desired to live. When an opportunity to make the shift was presented to me, I took it. I didn't hesitate. I set aside all logic and said, "*Yes!* The Universe is calling for me to move to the Carolinas." The job offer was far from a perfect opportunity. In fact, it was the most unstable offer I had ever received, but my heart would not allow me to hear anything other than, "It's time."

My life in Florida became more and more challenging. I could no longer just keep the peace in my relationship, or in my relationships with coworkers. I felt like a teakettle steamed up so hot it was ready to burst. Everything that had previously bothered me a little now felt intolerable.

I was simply no longer a match to the paradigm in which I had been living. This happens once we connect to our heart's desire and blow our breath of life into it—our paradigms will shift.

There are two ways we can handle this paradigm shift. The first, which is typical for many, is to swiftly clutch onto the old paradigm, frightened to the core of change. We suddenly change our mind because we don't want to lose the job, the partner, the friendship, the security, or whatever good we still see in our current situation. We make excuses for our difficult paradigm regardless of how uncomfortable it has become. We come up with ways to make it better.

The second way to handle our paradigm shift requires us to take a leap of faith and just do it. Know that the desire would not be in your heart if there wasn't support being perfectly and divinely aligned for you. Pray for grace throughout the entire experience. Toss out the lists and spreadsheets that show you the logical path, and follow the path of your heart!

There is no mistake no matter which path we choose! All paths lead to the same end. It is impossible to miss out on our lives. Our lives are ours to define and ours to make real. We will still experience the life lessons aligned for us because each path provides alternate opportunities for learning. It comes down to a matter of choosing which paradigm we want to live. If we take the first path, either the paradigm will become so intolerable we will shift, or we will have convinced our heart to be redirected, and our current paradigm may change. In my research, however, I have observed that, once people awaken to the desire within their hearts, it is simply a matter of time and how they choose to react to the shifts that occur.

Once we shift into alignment, it feels as if we are living a little bit of heaven on earth. Absolutely everything falls miraculously into place. We breathe more clearly and more fully. We desire to grow with much more grace, and grace is what we find. We find ourselves living a prosperous life and thriving. Once we understand how this process works, there is no going back to being "unconscious." Now that we "know," it becomes easier to connect to our heart's desire. We can blow our breath of life into our visions and allow our paradigms to shift.

Before we proceed any further, we must also know of the ultimate "shadow boxer"—the ego. The ego serves many purposes, but it is known best for its modus operandi (MO): it creates anxiety and doubt by convincing us of all the ways we could fail, or how things might go wrong. If we listen too closely to our ego, we run in endless circles and engage in self-flagellation. To combat the ego, we must first recognize its dwelling place.

CHAPTER 9

Awareness of Where Our Ego Is Dwelling

There are so many teachings about the ego. Here is a simple definition of the ego: "the part of us that causes constant worrying and that works to convince us of limitations that exist only in the mind." I love how Dr. Wayne Dyer describes the ego in his movie, *The Shift: Taking Your Life from Ambition to Meaning*: Ego means "Edging God Out" (Dyer 2010). This makes complete sense because our heart's desire is aligned with God. The ego separates us from our heart's desire with thoughts and emotions of limitation and worry.

If we were to break our lives down into areas of struggle, we would see there are basically five categories in which we are either thriving or striving:

1. Health
2. Career and finance
3. Love

4. Home
5. Spirituality and religion

I have always been fascinated that some people absolutely thrive in matters of money. They always have money. They work the best jobs, have great success, live in country club settings, and display other attributes of financial security. It appears that they haven't ever experienced financial lack. However, when I spend time with them, I find that they are often challenged in some other area such as love, health, or home.

Some people I have connected with really struggle in matters of love and relationships. They have a constant desire to meet a soul mate, be in love, get married, and live happily ever after. On the other side of the spectrum are people who are always in the best marriages and relationships. Love and happiness in relationships just seem to happen for them all the time. Another example are people who struggle greatly with health versus people who are always healthy and appear to never worry about anything when it comes to their health.

In observing these things, I have witnessed that everyone I have connected with appears to thrive in one or more areas while struggling in the others. Whatever area they struggle in—health, career and finance, love, home, or spirituality and religion—that is the area they try to manifest using the law of attraction in the way they understand it. Perhaps using prayer, affirmations, or vision boards, they mistakenly focus on the area in which they believe they are lacking, and therefore they get caught in a vicious cycle of attempting to achieve, missing, and attempting again to the point of frustration. The key here is to come to awareness that their experience of lack is ultimately a consequence of operating from that paradigm. I have developed a theory: To combat this cycle, we must simply shift our focus to the area of struggle with the exact same expectation we have in the areas in which we thrive. Only then will we will be able to master this process.

Personally, I have always thrived in the areas of love and home. I've always owned a home I love living in. There hasn't ever been an experience of lack in this area. Even when my spouse and I purchased the home of my dreams, it was a simple and fun process. I just knew all along it would happen. I got clear on what I wanted, wrote it down, and the next day we stumbled upon it. After we called the realtor, saw the home, and made our offer, we went to the house we were temporarily renting and packed. We wrote on our calendar the date we intended to move, and we acted as though that was the reality. It was so much fun to get a call that our closing was the day before the date on our calendar, and we moved on the date we had written. We harnessed our power. We knew what it was we wanted, and we moved forward with it. We didn't talk about it to everyone or create obsessive affirmations about it; we just did it.

It has been the same for me with love. I have always loved deeply, and I have always been loved. I have always simply known I would be with the person I loved and we would live happily. I have had two relationships. My first lasted nearly eleven years, and during that time, we were happy. The end of our relationship wasn't what I would call a drawn out, dramatic process; it was simple. We had grown apart in our respective journeys and agreed to part ways as friends. Within a year of moving from my life in Florida, I met my soul mate. Within a year of connecting, we were married. What was fun was that, right after we were married, the Supreme Court ruled that my marriage was legal! It's as though the Universe was simply waiting for me to take that step.

Even when I was single, I didn't obsess over wanting and not having the perfect marriage. Something within me simply knew it would happen. It has been the same with friendships; I've simply always known I would have great friendships. The knowing is so strong that I haven't ever thought about it.

In health, I have always known I would be healthy, for the most part. I know I need to eat nourishing foods and exercise regularly. I don't stress over body imbalances or fear about diagnoses. Even while I had an inner knowing of a possible diagnosis, I simply refocused my energy and balanced what I intuitively knew to balance.

Career and finance—this is the area that has always been a struggle of limitation for me. I have always wanted to have a successful career and financial stability. I have written affirmations, attended prosperity classes, prayed, meditated, applied divine teachings, and yet I have continued to struggle. I have taken the advice of financially successful people and yet still didn't achieve success. I always experienced getting a job that paid less than what I wanted. I got familiar with living paycheck to paycheck. I continued following the concept of borrowing from Peter to pay Paul, which I had learned as a child. I tried Psych K® (a way of accessing the subconscious mind), Ho'oponopono (a Hawaiian practice of reconciliation and forgiveness), hypnotism, past-life regressions, Reiki, crystal therapy, and more … on and on and on.

The light finally switched on for me, and it shined directly on my ego. This is where my ego hides—in the career and finance areas of my life. The awareness of where my ego hides gave me the power to surrender. A great teacher once told me, "It's funny we claim to have faith in the God of our understanding, yet we keep asking God/the Divine/the Universe for the same thing over and over, communicating that we don't actually believe we will be answered." Once I realized where my ego was hiding, and that I was doing the very thing that my great teacher said, I let it all go. I stopped asking. I changed my focus to simply being present in my life and being grateful. When my "ego" would pop up with thoughts of, "But maybe I need to ask it this way," or "Try that technique," I would smile, shake my head, and say, "Thank you, God, for showing me that I am already aligned. I am so grateful."

By surrendering, we move out of our own way. We align ourselves fully with the life we want. All of our prayers are answered in miraculous ways. We are completely taken care of. It's quite fun seeing the full manifestation because it comes in ways we may not have ever have imagined. Perhaps that is why the teachings of the law of attraction repeat that the *how* is none of our business!

CHAPTER 10

Holding It

An important key I have learned is the power of holding it—holding the desire close to my heart without sharing it with others. Our paradigms will shift when we have connected with our heart's desire and blown our breath of life into it. We will see changes occurring, and there will be indications it manifesting. This key is vitally important to experiencing our heart's desire: don't tell anyone about it!

The excitement of connecting with our desire and seeing hints of it coming to pass can create a deep eagerness to share this experience with our closest friends, family members, and loved ones. We may want to share it with coworkers or neighbors. The problem is that sharing this experience will cause that divine energy of creation to become exposed to others, which may, inadvertently, add to or subtract from the creation.

Let's say you connected to the heart's desire to be in a new career aligned with what you are passionate about. Once you share this with a coworker, who loves working with you, he or she may say, "Oh, I would hate to see you go." That just creates a block. Minor as it may be, it will slow the process. Another example could be your desire to buy a house or relocate. If you tell a neighbor or a friend nearby, he or she may feel excited for you but not want you to leave. Again, this will slow the process of manifestation.

It is fun to play a game of holding your desire within you. It will add to the energy of the creative forces, especially when your desire is almost in full manifestation. Once it has been fully created, and you now live that heart's desire, the excitement of sharing will decrease, as you will have become a vibrational match to that which you desire.

CHAPTER 11

Case Studies

N ow that I have recounted my personal experiences of obtaining my heart's desire, I'd like to repeat the meditation from the beginning of this book to help you discover your own. Please, get comfortable, and let us begin our journey from a place of Love. We will begin with the Heart's Desire Meditation.

Heart's Desire Meditation:

Close your eyes for a moment. Take in a deep breath and relax. Breathe in and count to four. Hold the breath and count to four. Now, breathe out and count to four. Do this twice. Now return to a normal breathing pattern.

Bring your awareness to your head and allow your head to simply relax. Bring your awareness to your shoulders and arms and feel them relax. Now, bring your awareness to your back, allowing your back to relax. Bring your awareness to your chest and then your abdomen and feel your upper torso relax. Bring your awareness down to your legs and feet. Allow your legs and feet to simply relax.

Now imagine you are walking down a beautiful path in nature. The temperature is perfect, and there is beauty all around you. The sounds of the birds are like a beautiful song. The sky is a bright blue, and the colors around you are brilliant and vivid. Notice up ahead there is a beautiful flowing waterfall and a perfect space for you to sit and relax. As you sit comfortably there, take in a loving breath from your heart. Now imagine in front of you an image of your heart. Feel his or her presence. Ask, "What is my truest heart's desire?" Listen for the answer.

As you breathe in the answer, feel the loving presence around you. Feel the powerful energy of love surrounding you. Experience what it would be like to live in your heart's desire. Allow that energy to grow around you.

Now, while maintaining that feeling, thank your heart for sharing this gift with you. Continue to carry that feeling with you as you begin your journey back. As you retrace your steps back down that beautiful trail in nature, feel the sense of gratitude for this time. Hold that love in your heart and when you are ready, open your eyes.

Write down everything you experienced. What is your heart's desire? How did you feel about being in your heart's desire? Did it excite you? Did it place a smile upon your face? Is there a part of you that felt childlike again, as if you were tapping into your imagination? In contrast, is there a part of you that said, "I wish," "If only I had … "That would be great if …"

Welcome to your heart's desire!

If you did not understand clearly your heart's desire, let go of any discouragement and simply continue to practice the meditation. You will understand it in perfect divine time.

Case Studies

Before I close, I would like to offer five case studies, each of which provides an inspiring example of how individuals have discovered their heart's desire and then embarked on a journey to make their desires manifest. I encountered these people in 2014 during a workshop I offered: "Living our Heart's Desire—Creating Heaven on Earth." Within one year of that intense workshop, I observed as the lives of these five participants powerfully unfolded into their heart's desires. So, here I offer the stories of how they obtained their heart's desires. I hope these stories broaden your understanding. Of course, I've used fictitious nicknames to protect their privacy. Here are the participants and their desires:

- Serena: To uplift humanity through teaching and inspiring others to connect to the light that is within them, and to truly live from that space.
- Tammy: To have more likeminded friends, and to one day be a yoga instructor.
- Jennifer: To confidently step into her gift as a medium and help solve missing-persons crimes.
- Cathy: To have an herbal store and grow herbs herself.
- Trinity: To live a life of abundance while being of service to the Divine and to manifest more love in the world.

Serena

During this workshop, Serena connected to the realization that she no longer wanted to walk in the shoes of another. She hoped to uplift humanity through teaching and inspiring others to connect to the light that is within them and to truly live from that space. She realized she no longer wanted to exhaust her energy by focusing it into what others wanted her to do.

Following the workshop, she breathed her breath of life into this realization by talking more about her desire. Up to this point, she had been lovingly leading a church to the best of her ability. She had also been taking care of another spiritual organization. She had realized during this workshop that these were two areas that felt intense and very much like burdens she was carrying. Truly stepping into her own desire to provide healing, teaching, and counseling and to make a decent salary doing so made her heart race with joy. She talked more and more about what she desired. As she continued to breathe that breath, her life circumstances changed.

Within one month of the workshop, a healing opportunity appeared between her and the widow of her teacher. After exchanging some loving e-mails, they met and engaged in a lengthy hug and some tears. Over a meal they spent a great deal of time sharing, apologizing, and forgiving in the deepest way. After this meeting, Serena passed the church where it was always destined to be. She felt she was simply a bridge, holding this space to provide time for the widow to heal. She lovingly released the church, knowing it was no longer hers to run.

In a year's time, Serena lovingly released her role in the other organization where she had been running the daily operations. She came to a deep realization that she had been living the pattern she had created when she was a child of doing what others needed her to do. In this pattern, she felt it was her obligation to complete life missions of others.

Today she has a prosperous new career that provides her with opportunities to counsel and reach people she may not have reached before. She has a thriving ministry in which she offers teaching, counseling, and healing. She has a job that fully aligns with her talents, and she receives support and financial means that are in balance. Today she is thriving in every area of her life—home, health, relationships, as well as finances and career.

Tammy

Tammy attended the 2014 Soul Journeys workshop. Upon completing the meditation, and as the day unfolded, she realized that she desired peace and direction in her life. Throughout much of her life, she had been seeking these things outside of herself. This is a characteristic so many people share. We seek that which we truly desire outside ourselves.

Breathing her breath of life into this awareness brought about many additional realizations and deep personal growth. Within three months, she identified all the aspects of her life that had brought her to the circumstances she was living. She directed her energy into yoga and meditation, which took her to the depths of her roots. Within six months, she unexpectedly returned to the place she was born. Within a year's time, she lived on the same street where she first lived and had spent her adolescence. All of these were opportunities to face unresolved past conflicts she had carried within her. Her life had become like a fast-moving river constantly shifting with unexpected turns. Each of these shifts and turns represented returning to a place where stagnant and unresolved energy still sat. The rapid waters came through, clearing out all of the energetic "muck."

Today, Tammy is back to where her soul journey in life began. She has faced, healed, and transcended many wounds. Like the Phoenix rising from the ashes, she has powerfully stepped into her light. Her deep and profound realization through all of this is that the peace and direction she was seeking in her life was within her the entire time. Her magnificent, yearlong journey led her to a place where she no longer experienced anxiety or fear. She is truly in her power now. When not working in her career, she spends her days training for and running marathons, doing hot yoga, and other physical training. She coaches women on how to live healthier lifestyles. She challenges men and women to push past their own limitations by eating healthy foods and exceeding their fitness goals. She's the happiest in her life she has ever been.

Tammy recovers quickly now, if she does stumble a bit. She has gained the self-love and self-respect she needed to find her answers within and grow past any perceived challenges that come across her path.

When we empower ourselves to leap fully into our heart's desire, we step into our authentic selves and can preserver in all our live goals. Tammy gives us an example of that.

Jennifer

Jennifer always had the gift of seeing and hearing those who had crossed over. Since she was a child, this was within her. For most of her adult life, this was a gift she kept hidden deep within herself. There were only two close people in her life with whom she shared this secret gift. When she connected to her heart's desire, she realized that using her abilities as a psychic medium to help solve missing-person cases was what she truly wanted to do.

Within two months of the workshop, she breathed her breath of life into this realization, and opportunities came flooding to her doorway. She connected with a world-renowned medium who offered certification courses. In her practicing, Jennifer did more readings for others. I witnessed an incredible healing occur as Jennifer did a reading for a grieving mother whose daughter had passed on. This mother had been tormented after her daughter's death. Their relationship had been challenging, and they had argued over the daughter's addiction problem before her death. Jennifer brought the daughter in and shared loving messages with the mother. To this day, that mother is transformed completely from her experience during that one session.

Jennifer continued to open up and share her gifts with

others. Within a year, she came out publicly on her Facebook page. She took a true leap of faith in doing so as she had no idea how her friends, her husband's friends, or even their family members would respond. Many were very conservative in their views on spirituality, and this added to her reservations. As Jennifer would discover, when we step into our heart's desire, *we* not only thrive, but humanity thrives too. This was made evident when her gifts healed people from all over the world.

Today Jennifer is booked up to three months in advance for her readings. She is being trained one-on-one by a world-renowned psychic (name withheld for privacy). Once she breathed her breath of life into this desire, doors opened in ways that were beyond her expectations. Her practice is thriving, and all of her previous barriers have subsided.

Cathy

Cathy attended the first Soul Journeys workshop. She connected to her heart's desire through the meditation of the same name, and she gained much clarity throughout the day. She wanted to own her own herbal shop and offer organic foods from local farmers in her community. This was something she always knew she would love to do, and had said the words *one day* time and time again. Now she felt empowered and inspired to make her dream a reality.

Upon returning home, she breathed her breath of life into this desire with a renewed intensity. She held conversations with local community garden farmers about this desire. She found there was more support around her than she ever imagined. She was inspired to apply for a business loan. She worked on a business plan and submitted it to the lender and to the landlord of a vacant space in her community. The space was ideal—it had amazing character, and it fit perfectly with her vision. The landlord was equally excited. He shared her vision and vowed to support it, so much that he offered to reduce his original asking price. The loan was approved with ease.

In her heart's desire, Cathy envisioned success in her business, as well as support from her family. There was an important component to this case study. As things fell into place with ease, her family life began to shake up. She did not receive the support from her spouse at that time that she longed for. This caused her to clutch to the old paradigms while also blowing more breath of life into the new. These two were contrasting one another.

When our current lives don't match the lives we desire, a choice becomes imperative. There is no going back. Once we know and connect to our heart's desire, we experience it as a light that doesn't turn off.

Cathy continued to try to bring them both together. Ultimately, the relationship ended. The business, which had been thriving, had declined. The reason for this was missing a key: *Taking the leap of faith and letting go.*

Today Cathy is well on her way. Her personal life and professional life have healed greatly, and she is moving boldly forward. The important element to this study is that she didn't fail. She simply was unwilling to let go of what wasn't a match to the manifestation of all that she desired even though elements did not match. This was a key and a vital lesson for her to experience and offered a great teaching for many of us to learn from. When we connect with our heart's desire it is important to allow the unfolding with grace and love.

Trinity

Trinity embarked on a journey to the ministry. This was far from anything she ever thought she would do. However, a calling came to her heart after the death of her younger daughter. After the passing of her sweet daughter, Trinity's entire life changed. Her perspectives changed. Her heart's desire was pushing forward, ever present. Though she was unsure of how it would manifest, she knew that her heart desired to live a life of abundance in service to the Divine through healing and helping others. She also had a deep desire to manifest more love in the world. The last piece was in honor of her daughter's legacy.

At the beginning of her ministry studies, her mentor felt guided to help her remember the gifts that were within her— gifts she had long suppressed and never fully used. A light switched on as she recognized her heart's desire to help and heal others, a gift that is nothing less than spectacular. When she blew her breath of life into her heart's desire, opportunities flooded that allowed her to offer her gift of intuitive guidance. Every recipient of her readings shed a lifetime of healing tears, giving her the nickname "the crying medium."

Trinity made a most profound statement after she allowed her paradigm to shift and she stepped more fully into the light of who she is: "I always imagined that one would need to heal their 'stuff' before ever offering their gifts of healing to others. The truth I have learned is that by stepping fully into who I am and embracing all of my gifts, my 'stuff' healed instantly."

This is the truth about taking that leap of faith. When we take a leap of faith toward who we really are, our action transcends the time and space of healing. There is something spectacular about this journey.

Like the other individuals I had studied, Trinity had connected to her heart's desire. She is the most recent case study and is continuing to go through paradigm shifts. During this period of great transitional flux, only divine time will tell what will occur. One thing is for certain—once you are connected to your heart's desire, there is no turning back. The shifting may be challenging at times, but it will always catapult you into a life of thriving.

I could share so many more details for each of these stories. To keep the identity of these people private, I have chosen to offer only a synopsis of each story. I can share that each was studied and counseled over a time span of two years. Each followed the same guidance I have presented in this book. All are thriving in their lives today, as they continue to connect to their heart's desires and live the greatness of who they will be.

CHAPTER 12

Conclusion

Without exception, each and every one of us has the divine, God-given ability to live our lives in a way that leads us to thrive. We all can live lives that will make us happy and for which we can be grateful. We have the right and the ability to live what is within our hearts. We will experience in life whatever is in our hearts. This causes me to ponder. Perhaps this is the true meaning of the word *sin*, which in Aramaic translates to "missing the point." If we lived our lives ignoring that which we desire in our hearts, have we missed the point of life?

When we connect to our heart's desire, we feel ourselves surrounded by feelings of love. I venture to say that love is the meaning of life. Living "heaven on earth" is a powerful experience, and we are all here for that experience. All it takes is a simple process of connecting to our heart's desire, blowing our breath of life into that desire, allowing our paradigm to shift, and ultimately coming to the space of being.

Life is full of magic and mystery. If we choose, we can

experience joy and adventure, and we can live with childlike wonder by simply allowing life to unfold for us. There is no need to try to control our lives and our outcomes. We live, breathe, and operate in a very loving and supportive Universe. The ancient laws that operate the Universe work for us in ways we are just now beginning to understand. These laws are working with us whether we consciously know of it or not. I sometimes think about an old adage that I've heard most of my life: "The rich get richer while the poor keep getting poorer." This is the result of these universal laws working in full force and effect. The current perception of the widening gap between socioeconomic groups is due, in large part, to where we have been focusing our energy.

If I am constantly focusing on being unhappy in my current circumstance, that is what I will continue to experience. When I choose to focus on my heart's desire and use the tools I understand, my current circumstance will change.

Within each of us is the divine blueprint to our lives. Everything we see outside of ourselves reflects that which is within us. When we gaze up into the infinite, expansive Universe and see the unfathomable beauty that exists above us, we are seeing a mere refection of the unfathomable beauty within us. When we connect with the truth of who we are, we are more powerful than we could ever have imagined ourselves to be. The soul's journey is the journey of living heaven on earth. What does heaven on earth look like to each of us? Every desire within our heart is a brick in the foundation of our mansions, the garden in our yards, and the window of our souls. Within us is the perfection of our lives. We hold all answers to all the questions in our hearts. The first step to living heaven on earth is to connect to our heart's desire.

The soul's journey is a brilliant masterpiece. It is filled with excitement, hope, faith, and frustrations, disappointments, and tragedy. Every experience we have in our journey beckons us to go within and connect back to that divine blueprint. We may not see the entire view, but our heart's desire will give us just what we need in perfect divine time.

Reference list

Schucman, Helen, ed. 2007. *A Course In Miracles: Combined Volume 3rd Edition*. California: The Foundation for Inner Peace.

Andrews, Ted. 2007. *Animal Speak: The Spiritual and Magical Powers of Creatures Great and Small*. Minnesota: Llewellyn Publications.

Byrne, Rhonda. 2006. *The Secret*. New York: Simon & Schuster, Inc.

Behrend, Genevieve. 1951. *Your Invisible Power*. California: DeVorss & Company.

Braden, Gregg. 2009. *Fractal Time: The Secret of 2012 and a New World Age*. California: Hay House, Inc.

Butterworth, Eric. 2001. *Spiritual Economics: The Principles and Process of True Prosperity*. Missouri: Unity Books.

Dyer, Wayne W. 2009. *Excuses Begone!: How to change lifelong, self-defeating thinking habits*. California: Hay House, Inc.

Dyer, Wayne W. 2007. *Change Your Thoughts, Change Your Life: Living the Wisdom of the Tao.* California: Hay House, Inc.

Dyer, Wayne W. 2006. *Inspiration: Your Ultimate Calling.* California: Hay House, Inc.

Errico, Rocco A. 1994. *Let There Be Light: The Seven Keys.* Texas: The Noohra Foundation.

Errico, Rocco A. 1998. *And There Was Light.* Texas: The Noohra Foundation.

Gerber, Richard, M.D. 1998. *Vibrational Medicine: The #1 Handbook of Subtle-Energy Therapies.* Vermont: Bear and Company.

Hicks, Esther, and Hicks, Jerry. 2004. *Ask and It Is Given: Learning to Manifest Your Desires.* California: Hay House, Inc.

Hicks, Esther, and Hicks, Jerry. 2006. *The Law of Attraction: The Basics of the Teachings of Abraham.* California: Hay House, Inc.

Hopfe, Lewis M. and Woodward, Mark R. 1998. *Religions of the World.* New Jersey: Prentice Hall, Inc.

Hopkins, Emma Curtis. 1951. *Self Treatments including The Radiant I Am.* Wise Woman Press. Oregon: Wise Woman Press.

Khalsa, Dharma Singh, MD. 2005. *The End of Karma: 40 Days to Perfect Peace, Tranquility, and Joy.* California: Hay House, Inc.

Rasha, 2003. *Oneness: The Teachings.* New Mexico: Earth Star Press.

Schucman, Helen, ed. 2007. *A Course In Miracles: Combined Volume 3rd Edition.* California: The Foundation for Inner Peace.

Selwa, Barbara. *Ever Closer, Even Closer, and Ministerial Book.* North Carolina: The Alliance of Divine Love, Inc.

Selwa, Barbara. 2003. *The Doorway to the Ultimate Seeing: A Doctoral Workbook.* North Carolina: The Alliance of Divine Love, Inc.

Smoley, Richard. 2002. *Inner Christianity: A Guide to the Esoteric Tradition.* Colorado: Shambhala Publications, Inc.

Tolle, Eckhart. 1999. *The Power of Now: A Guide to Spiritual Enlightenment.* California: Namaste Publishing and New World Library.

The Way of Mastery. 2012. California: Shanti Christo Foundation.

CPSIA information can be obtained
at www.ICGtesting.com
Printed in the USA
LVOW12*0223101117

555746LV00002B/8/P